ETHICAL LEADERSHIP
AND DECISION MAKING
IN EDUCATION
Applying Theoretical Perspectives
to Complex Dilemmas

TOPICS IN EDUCATIONAL LEADERSHIP

Larry W. Hughes, Series Editor

ETHICAL LEADERSHIP
AND DECISION MAKING
IN EDUCATION
Applying Theoretical Perspectives
to Complex Dilemmas

Joan Poliner Shapiro
Temple University

Jacqueline A. Stefkovich
The Pennsylvania State University

LAWRENCE ERLBAUM ASSOCIATES, PUBLISHERS
2001   Mahwah, New Jersey   London

Lawrence Erlbaum Associates, Inc., Publishers
10 Industrial Avenue
Mahwah, New Jersey 07430

Cover design by Kathryn Houghtaling Lacey

Library of Congress Cataloging-in-Publication Data

Shapiro, Joan Poliner
    Ethical leadership and decision making in education : applying theoretical
perspectives to complex dilemmas / Joan Poliner Shapiro, Jacqueline A. Stefkovich.
        p.   cm.
    Includes bibliographical references and index.
    ISBN 0-8058-3250-5 (p)
        1. Educational leadership—Moral and ethical aspects—United States.
2. School administrators—Professional ethics—United States.   3. School
management and organization—Moral and ethical aspects—United States.
4. Ethics—Study and teaching—United States.   5. Decision making—
United States.   I. Stefkovich, Jacqueline Anne. 1947– II. Title.
LB1738.5.S52   2000
371.2′011—dc21   00-027985
                                                                              CIP

Books published by Lawrence Erlbaum Associates are printed on acid-free paper,
and their bindings are chosen for strength and durability.

Printed in the United States of America
10   9   8   7   6   5   4   3   2   1

In memory of my mother, Ruth P. Poliner,
and sister, Dr. Elizabeth A. Poliner—
both were exemplars of the ethic of care

A special thanks to my parents,
Albert and Betty Stefkovich,
whose values have always
inspired my work

Contents

Preface

The impetus for writing this book came from three developments in the field of educational leadership: (a) a burgeoning interest in the study of ethics among educational leaders, (b) a rising tendency to use case studies as a method of reflection on administrative problems, and (c) the development of new licensure standards for school leaders that require an understanding of ethical issues.

Keeping these developments in mind, this preface addresses the purposes of this book, what this book contains, how it is organized, and how the information provided fills a gap in the educational leadership knowledge base. Also included is a brief introduction to the instructor who decides to teach a course using this book and acknowledgments to those who have been helpful in seeing this work through to its publication.

PURPOSE OF THIS BOOK

This book has several purposes. First, it demonstrates the application of different ethical paradigms through the discussion and analysis of real-life moral dilemmas. Second, it addresses some of the practical, pedagogical, and curricular issues related to the teaching of ethics for educational leaders. Third, it emphasizes the importance of ethics instruction from a variety of theoretical approaches. Finally, this book provides a process that instructors might follow to develop their own ethics unit or course.

CONTENTS AND ORGANIZATION

This book discusses how students and practitioners should take into account each of four paradigms presented (i.e., the ethic of justice, the ethic of care, the ethic of critique, and the ethic of the profession) to help solve authentic dilemmas. We have structured these dilemmas with key questions to assist the readers to think in ways that they may not have considered in the past.

These questions may also help to open the minds of students, practitioners, or both when introduced to the four paradigms in the book. If they are presented as options, these paradigms may help students and practitioners better solve complex dilemmas in today's challenging and diverse society.

Part I, the first two chapters of this book, provides an overview of why ethics is so important, especially for today's educational leaders, and describes a multi-paradigm approach essential to practitioners as they grapple with ethical dilemmas.

Part II deals with the dilemmas themselves. After a brief introduction as to how the cases were constructed, an illustration is provided of how the multiparadigm approach may be applied to a real dilemma. This example is followed by chapters 3 through 7, which contain ethical dilemmas written by graduate students. These are the kinds of dilemmas faced by practicing administrators in urban, suburban, and rural settings in an era full of complexities and contradictions.

Part III focuses on pedagogy. Chapter 8 provides teaching notes to the instructor. To do this, we, as professors and authors,[1] discuss the importance of self-reflection on the part of instructors as well as students. We model how we thought through our own personal and professional ethical codes as well as reflected on the critical incidents in our lives that shaped our teaching and frequently determined what we privileged or emphasized in class.

THE CASE STUDY APPROACH TO TEACHING ETHICS

The case study approach to teaching educators has garnered considerable interest in the past few years. Much of this interest has been stimulated by educational theories focusing on the merits of reflective practice (Dewey, 1902) and prompted by the successful use of cases for the training of business leaders, an effort spearheaded by Harvard University's Business School. Indeed, Nash (1996), in his book on professional ethics, pointed out that: "A good case can be a provocative, almost indispensable tool for teaching the relevant moral concepts . . ." (p. 64). In response to this interest, a number of authors have written case books aimed at teaching (Cooper, 1995; Goodlad, Soder, & Sirotnik, 1990; Greenwood & Fill-

---

[1]The authorship of this book is in alphabetical order. Both authors contributed equally to the writing of this book.

mer, 1997; Strike & Soltis, 1992) and at general aspects of educational administration (Ashbaugh & Kasten, 1995; Kirschmann, 1996; Merseth, 1997; Willower
& Licata, 1997). A few others have written texts on cases in ethics aimed at a general population (e.g., Glaser, 1994).

There are also a number of fine scholarly ethics books aimed at educational administrators (e.g., Beck, 1994; Starratt, 1994a). In 1988, Strike, Haller, and Soltis
combined a scholarly approach with cases to present a textbook of ethical dilemmas aimed specifically at the problems faced by educational administrators. Their
approach to ethics has been primarily from a justice perspective.

In the past few years, there has been a resurgence of interest in, and recognition
of the importance of, ethics for educational administrators. Here, the justice perspective has been joined by other approaches, namely those of care and critique.
Additionally, the profession of educational leadership has recognized a need for
ethics competencies. Such developments have exposed gaps in the knowledge
base that cry out for a response.

GAPS IN THE KNOWLEDGE BASE

The idea for this book germinated over a 9-year period during which we taught
ethics to diverse educational leaders. During this time, we came to realize the
dearth of materials available for our training. We advocate reflective practice and,
thus, saw the benefits of including a case study approach as part of our instruction.
However, most of the case books we could find either focused broadly on educators in general and did not consider the unique problems of educational leaders,
centered on educational administrators but not on ethical issues, or did both but
only discussed ethics primarily from a justice perspective (Strike, Haller, &
Soltis, 1988).

Viewing ethics through different paradigms is a relatively recent phenomenon.
Hence, to our knowledge, no texts have been developed that discuss ethical dilemmas from multiple perspectives (i.e., to include the ethics of care and critique as
well as justice). Moreover, although many are concerned with issues of professional ethics, none has grappled with the concept of professional ethics as a separate paradigm.

Thus, we see this book as complementing others that have gone before it by
filling a real gap in the knowledge base of ethics training for educational administrators. It provides a conceptual model for the analysis of professional ethics and
then includes dilemmas and questions designed to stimulate discussion, taking
into account the ethics of justice, care, critique, and the profession.

We believe our approach is an authentic one, incorporating the voices of our
students and using dilemmas they have developed in our classes. We believe that
this approach, although a bit unorthodox, responds to Nash's (1996) concerns and
observations when he said, "The difficulty I have with some textbook cases . . . is

that they are oftentimes so overly dramatic they make no claim to verisimilitude. . . . I have found over the years that the best provenance for cases is in my students' own work lives" (p. 64).

Finally, we believe there is merit in providing a process by which professors and practitioners alike can come to grips with their own ethical codes and then apply these codes to practical situations—something that no one has done to date.

TEACHING NOTES TO THE INSTRUCTOR

We have taken considerable time to design this book so that it can be easily used for instructional purposes. In chapter 2, we give an overview of multiple ethical perspectives that instructors might wish to present to the students. Additionally, in each of the chapters that contain ethical dilemmas, we offer a series of questions to assist the instructor in facilitating the discussion of each dilemma.

In the teaching of ethics, we not only ask instructors to help students reflect on their own personal values and professional beliefs, but we strongly encourage instructors to do the same. We believe it is imperative that we *all* become reflective practitioners when attempting to solve ethical dilemmas. We do not advocate one best way to accomplish this task, but we do provide some detailed information in chapter 8 as to how we have taught ethics to our students by engaging in a process of self-reflection. We not only invite instructors to read this chapter but we hope students find this section of interest as well.

We have also designed this book so that it is easily adaptable for a variety of uses with a wide range of audiences. It can be used either as a basic or supplementary text for university courses related to the preparation of educational leaders, including, but not limited to, principals, superintendents, curriculum coordinators, personnel administrators, and business administrators. It is appropriate for either introductory or advanced levels of educational administration programs and could be infused into almost all of the educational administration curriculum or taught in a discrete ethics course.

This book would also provide an excellent professional reference for aspiring and practicing school administrators, central office personnel, educational policy makers, state department personnel, and regional and federal level education staff. Others interested in the book as a reference might include school board members, parents' organizations, and professional associations. Moreover, we do not see this case book as limited to the United States; professionals working in other countries have responded positively to the dilemmas we have presented.

ACKNOWLEDGMENTS

We thank Naomi Silverman from Lawrence Erlbaum Associates, Publishers for her helpful and insightful suggestions. We also thank the following reviewers who provided worthwhile and useful feedback: William P. Foster, University of Indiana; William D. Greenfield, Portland State University; Larry W. Hughes, University of Houston; Sharon D. Kruse, University of Akron; Nel Noddings, Stanford University; and H. Svi Shapiro, University of North Carolina, Greensboro. We appreciate the work of all our student contributors, but are especially grateful to the lead authors in each of the dilemma chapters—Patricia A. L. Ehrensal, James Krause, G. Michaele O'Brien, Leon Poeske, and Deborah Weaver. Not only did they contribute through their writing, but they spent endless hours coordinating the work of their co-contributors into a coherent chapter.

In addition, we appreciate all the valuable input from the following: Temple University's Educational Leadership & Policy Studies (ELPS) 1998 and 1999 doctoral cohorts who piloted earlier drafts of our cases; Lynn Cheddar and Robert D. McCaig, ELPS doctoral students, for their preliminary editing; and all our students who, throughout the years, have helped us not only to formulate our professional ethical paradigm but who have helped us to grow as professionals and as human beings.

I

PRACTICE AND PARADIGMS IN THE STUDY OF ETHICS

Part I sets the stage for exploring and solving the ethical dilemmas that make up a central portion (Part II) of this book. It serves as an introduction and consists of chapters 1 and 2.

Chapter 1 offers a brief discussion of the multiple ethical paradigm approach and its importance in view of the complexities and diversity of this current era. It incorporates the voices of our students, who support our assertion that the study of ethics is needed for all school leaders, particularly in light of changes in society. This chapter explores implications for practice and for programs aimed at the preparation of educational leaders.

Chapter 2 describes the conceptual framework underlying our teaching and scholarship in the area of ethics. Here, we stress the importance of training for educational leaders in the ethics of justice, care, and critique. To these, we add a fourth ethic, that of the profession. It is in this chapter that we explain our framework for understanding and using this ethic. The discussion of the four paradigms is meant to encourage the reader to deal with the ethical dilemmas that follow in Part II in a multidimensional way.

We believe it is important to try out diverse approaches for the solving of ethical cases even for those of us who usually respond to dilemmas as moral absolutists or as moral relativists. Practice in working through a multidimensional paradigm process should provide current and future educational leaders with options for dealing with complex and difficult ethical dilemmas that they will face daily.

1

Multiple Ethical Paradigms and the Preparation of Educational Leaders in a Diverse and Complex Era

> *Of all the courses I have taken, at all levels, this course has no boundaries.*
> *What I mean is all the materials we have read, the discussions we have had*
> *and the lessons I have learned, directly impact all I will study and all I will*
> *do.... Ethics courses should not be only for students who are interested in*
> *going on to law school or medical school. [They] should be for students who*
> *are interested in becoming citizens.... If anyone ever challenges the rele-*
> *vance of a course such as this in an educational leadership curriculum, [he*
> *or she is] not an educated individual.*
> —Graduate student in educational leadership

Foster (1986) expressed the seriousness and importance of ethics in educational administration when he wrote, "Each administrative decision carries with it a restructuring of human life: that is why administration at its heart is the resolution of moral dilemmas" (p. 33). In this paradoxical and ethically polarized era, we began to think that there was a need to offer differing perspectives to help educational administrators solve real-life dilemmas that they frequently face in their schools and in their communities.

In this chapter, we discuss the complexities of this era particularly as they relate to schools and leadership in an increasingly diverse society. We also discuss why ethical leadership is needed especially as we move toward the next millennium. We then introduce a multiple ethical paradigm approach to assist educational leaders in grappling with complexities and diversity. This section ends with comments relative to the training of practitioners. Throughout this discussion, we emphasize the voices of our numerous and diverse graduate students, many of

3

whom indicate support and provide a basis for our belief that the teaching of ethics is critical in the preparation of educational leaders.

ETHICAL LEADERSHIP IN A COMPLEX
AND DIVERSE SOCIETY

In the 21st century, as society becomes even more demographically diverse, educational administrators will, more than ever, need to be able to develop, foster, and lead tolerant and democratic schools. We believe that, through the study of ethics, educational leaders of tomorrow will be better prepared to recognize, reflect on, and appreciate differences. This need for ethical preparation is perhaps best expressed by our own graduate students, most of whom are practitioners in public schools.

Consider the words of this woman, who, in her journal, described the essence of this need by writing about some of the scandals of the 1990s involving high-ranking government officials, rock stars, and athletes. Her words captured our imaginations mainly because of their empowering effect on school administrators. She wrote:

> Given this admittedly bleak picture of life in the not-so-moral America of the 90s, it does not seem hyperbolic to say that we, as educators and administrators in our nation's schools, may well be part of an ever-dwindling group of citizens who continue to form a bastion against the growing phenomenon of unethical behavior in our country. How then could a program aimed at preparing men and women to serve as administrators in our nation's educational institutions possibly be considered complete without the inclusion of a course that requires would-be pedagogical leaders to examine both their personal and professional ethics and the impact that their ethical codes will have on their day-to-day administrative decision making?

Likewise, many of our students made direct connections between what was taught in our ethics class and the importance of diversity. Here, we use a broad-based definition of *diversity* that encompasses cultural categories of race/ethnicity, religion, social class, gender, disability, and sexual orientation as well as individual differences taking into account learning styles, exceptionalities, and age (Banks & Banks, 1993; Cushner, McClelland, & Safford, 1992; Gollnick & Chinn, 1994; Shapiro, Sewell, & DuCette, 1995; Sleeter & Grant, 1988).

As one of our students, a White, male biology professor in a rural setting, pointed out:

> I believe that there is strength in diversity. Diverse biological ecosystems are more stable, might this also be true of social systems? How can we prevent institutions from co-opting women and other minorities and instead cherish the diversity they provide? As educators we must strive to foster diversity as a source of variability en-

abling our society to adapt and contribute constructively in a rapidly changing world.

During our teaching of ethics, we also began to recognize that diversity was not just across students, but within each group of students as well. For example, our classes contained a number of Black students; yet, in some instances, race seemed to be their only commonality. Although of the same race, some of these students were male and others were female. Some were in their 20s, whereas others were closer to 50. Some were African-American; others were from non-American countries. Some were from urban areas; others lived and worked in suburbia. Some came from poverty, others from affluence. Therefore, many of the perspectives that these students of color held were not race-bound, but were influenced just as much or more by demographics, culture, age, or gender or by a combination of these factors.

Illustrative of this concept is a comment from an African-American female who observed issues relative to age, race, and gender:

> It has been my experience that younger women in my classes think this feminist thing is blown out of proportion because they have not faced any of the glass ceilings society can impose. The historical perspective is essential in order that males and females have some basis for challenging themselves and their assumptions with respect to race and gender. Perhaps the humanistic, caring leader is the answer, or at least the best possibility on the horizon. Politics and social reforms have not solved the problem, so educators—with the eventual help of parents—must.

Similarly, division across gender lines was not always the case. In all of our classes, there were often differences of opinion between women, with some taking a more traditional justice perspective and others favoring feminist approaches such as those of Gilligan (1982) and Noddings (1984, 1992). And, there were always men who made sure the class understood that women did not corner the market on caring. A number of men and women alike asserted that caring was not gender specific, especially in professions such as education. As one such student said, "We are all in the caring business, so how can we not consider what is best for all people concerned in these situations?"

Religion, too, in combination with other factors such as gender and age, influenced students' perceptions. Consider the comments of this White male teacher in his 30s who expressed his reactions on reading Gilligan's abortion dilemmas. He wrote:

> I found myself considering the different feelings that women must go through in considering an issue such as abortion. Even though my own personal belief is one that centers around my religious upbringing, I felt myself struggling with the decisions that had to be made.

Thus, in considering themes of diversity, we found that no one characteristic of students (e.g., race, gender, age, religion, professional experience, etc.) resulted in a monolithic view of ethics. Rather, students' views of ethics emanated from a combination of diverse factors and cut across lines of race and gender. This Black woman, a foreign student in her late 50s, summed up the importance of ethics in a diverse society when she presented this global, cross-cultural view:

> I think the effort of finding our voice(s) is going to continue for a long time, and it will also continue along lines of class, race, ethnicity, and other divisiveness; we will in no way speak with almost one voice until the pendulum swings again in the opposite direction. But with each shift we pick up more and more contentious issues.

But, perhaps this urban-based, African-American male best captured issues related to our complex and diverse society when he made this observation. Reflecting on personal liberty rather than the public good, he asked: "Who is the public? Who is the majority? And how do educational leaders fit into this scheme?" He described his dilemma this way:

> I work with a colleague who prides himself on being able to treat all of his students the same way. Regardless of race, economic status or ability, he claims to have the means to maintain a completely unbiased view on all. After working with him for six years, I have noticed that he does not have this ability. On a regular basis, I see him playing favorites, making exceptions, and generally doing the exact thing he claims he does not do. As an administrator, he cannot afford to be so rigid. There must be some room for partiality. And he shows it (though he would not admit to it) daily. It seems to me that this inability to be impartial grows out of his position and, in fact, would evolve from any position of administration when the interests of minorities and the oppressed have to be served. A 21st century administrator must be ready to bend, adjust and, when necessary, show partiality to those he/she serves if equity and justice are to be served.

This is only one illustration of the many types of paradoxes that educators must grapple with in making ethical decisions. To assist in analysis of such dilemmas, we advocate a multiparadigm approach that crosses over and combines various approaches to ethics.

THE IMPORTANCE OF A MULTIPLE PARADIGM APPROACH

Throughout this book, the reader is asked to consider current and challenging real-life ethical dilemmas using four paradigms. The four paradigms include the ethics of justice, critique, care, and the profession. Justice, critique, and care are familiar to many in the field of educational leadership.

All too often, however, professional ethics is seen as an extension of another paradigm and not thought to stand alone. That is why, in this book, we spend considerable time on the ethic of the profession rather than on the other three forms of ethics. We are convinced that this paradigm deserves to be treated as an independent model. We think that it is extremely important and complements the other paradigms.

We believe that it makes sense, when dealing with the ethic of the profession, for graduate students and/or practitioners to take the time to locate the formal codes of the profession and the standards of the field. Along with these activities, we strongly recommend that everyone write out personal and professional ethical codes and compare and contrast their two codes. In this way, educators can determine where consistencies exist between the codes and where clashes of codes might appear. These exercises lead to a much better understanding of "self" both as a professional and as a person.

The four perspectives or paradigms should help educational administrators solve real-life, complex dilemmas that they frequently face in their schools and in their communities. By using the different paradigms, educators should become aware of the perspective or perspectives they tend to use most often when solving ethical issues. For example, if an individual has a strong religious upbringing, then, depending on the religious persuasion, the ethic of justice with an emphasis on rights and laws may be the favored approach, or perhaps the ethic of care with its emphasis on compassion and empathy may be the paradigm of choice. And, as just mentioned, factors such as age, gender, race, or more likely a confluence of factors, may influence the paradigm one prefers.

However, despite any inclinations toward one perspective, the intent of this book is to ask graduate students, practitioners, or both, to open their minds by taking into account a variety of models, not simply one or two. Dilemmas in educational institutions can be complicated and may naturally lead to the use of two or more paradigms to solve problems. Today, with the complexity of situations and cultures, it seems more important than ever for educational leaders to think more broadly and go beyond "self" in an attempt to understand others.

In chapter 8, we discuss our own experiences of self-reflection to provide some concrete examples of this process. Learning to be self-reflective is not easy. It requires a concentrated effort on the part of individuals. This can be accomplished in privacy. It can also be encouraged in a staff development program or as part of an educational leadership preparation program.

THE PREPARATION OF ETHICAL EDUCATIONAL LEADERS

In many ways, the teaching of ethics diverges from the traditional paths employed by many educational administration programs. Although we do not necessarily advocate that standard courses be changed, we do believe that the teaching of ethics can be a welcome and important addition to those programs. As one of our students wrote in her class journal:

> This course has been very enlightening. It has been a thought-provoking break from the practical mundane courses of Educational Administration. . . . My vision has increased and multiplied. Even though I still view the world with racial vision, I am now more in tune with my feminist 'ear.' I will investigate, read and learn more and react more critically to my environment.

Others, through our classes, began to recognize the importance of ethics and its contribution to our larger society. This student, in particular, seemed to show a grasp of this bigger picture as it related to the issue of social justice:

> Social justice or equity really seems very obvious as a concept, but it apparently is necessary to make this topic a large part of the doctoral program because it is brought up so often in the readings and discussion. The result is that I am keenly aware of equity as an issue now and I doubt that I will look at such issues the same as before I started the doctoral program. It is hard to know exactly what my thoughts were about equity before I started the program. I really can't say because the awareness has come so gradually.

Clearly, the majority of students in our courses wanted ethics taught as part of the educational administration curriculum. In fact, there was no ambivalence in their wish that it be continued and even expanded as a disciplinary area in their program. This student's thoughts illustrate the types of comments that we have heard through the years:

> I feel it imperative for the administrator to be cognizant of . . . the need for institutions of higher learning to maintain a careful balance between those courses that are offered for some instrumental end and those which are offered merely for the sake of obtaining knowledge. I perceive that there is a greater societal pressure on the university for more of the former and less of the latter. We seem to place a much greater focus on acquiring knowledge for the sake of gaining employment than for the sheer joy of knowing. [Yet,] there is a special feeling, indescribable though it may be, in learning something that is new, different, and stimulating.

IN SUMMARY

In summary, in this book, we propose that there should not be one best ethical paradigm. Instead, we believe that by using different models, graduate students and practitioners will be able to work through their own personal and professional ethical codes, try out what they discovered about themselves by reflecting on the solutions they reach as they analyze diverse ethical dilemmas, and gain greater insights into the conceptual underpinnings of the ethical paradigm or paradigms they have chosen.

While analyzing the dilemmas in chapters 3 through 7, educational graduate students and/or practitioners should consciously reflect on the processes used to find solutions to cases. Along with the analysis related to a case, each individual should be able to do a great deal of reflection and soul-searching about his or her private code and professional code and should be open-minded enough to revise either of them as self-awareness and growth occur.

It is our hope that this book will empower school administrators to make wise decisions that seem appropriate to them and to others as leaders of educational institutions in a complex and contradictory era.

2

Viewing Ethical Dilemmas Through Multiple Paradigms

According to John Dewey (1902), *ethics* is the science that deals with conduct insofar as this is considered as right or wrong, good or bad. Ethics comes from the Greek word *ethos*, which means customs or usages, especially belonging to one group as distinguished from another. Later, ethics came to mean disposition or character, customs, and approved ways of acting. Looking at this definition from a critical perspective, one might ask: Ethics approved by whom? Right or wrong according to whom?

In this chapter, in an attempt to answer these and other important questions, we turn to three kinds of ethics emanating from diverse traditions that have an impact on education in general and educational leadership in particular. These paradigms include ethics from three viewpoints: justice, critique, and care. To these, we add a fourth model, that of the ethic of the profession. What follows is a broad overview of the ethics of justice, critique, and care and a more detailed explanation of the ethic of the profession.

Regarding the ethics of justice, critique, and care, we would like you to keep in mind that these are broad-based descriptions. Our intent for these three kinds of ethics is to provide enough of an introduction to the paradigms or models to enable you to receive a general sense of each of them. In an effort to be brief, we have had to leave out some outstanding scholars whose works are related to each of the paradigms. For in-depth coverage of scholars and their work regarding the ethics of justice, critique, and care, we suggest that you turn to our references in this book, locate other readings related to the models, and move beyond these introductory remarks.

In the case of the ethic of the profession, however, special attention is given to this paradigm. We do this because we believe there is a gap in the educational leadership literature in using the paradigm of professional ethics to help solve moral dilemmas. All too frequently, the ethic of the profession is seen as simply a part of the justice paradigm. We do not believe this is so, and we want to make the argument that this form of ethics can be used separately as a fourth lens for reflecting on, and then dealing with, dilemmas faced by educational leaders. Therefore, what we present in this chapter is a more involved discussion of the ethic of the profession than of the other three paradigms.

THE ETHIC OF JUSTICE

The ethic of justice focuses on rights and law and is part of a liberal democratic tradition that, according to Delgado (1995), "is characterized by incrementalism, faith in the legal system, and hope for progress" (p. 1). The liberal part of this tradition is defined as a "commitment to human freedom," and the democratic aspect implies "procedures for making decisions that respect the equal sovereignty of the people" (Strike, 1991, p. 415).

Starratt (1994a) described the ethic of justice as emanating from two schools of thought, one originating in the 17th century including the work of Hobbes and Kant, and more contemporary scholars such as Rawls and Kohlberg; the other rooted in the works of philosophers such as Aristotle, Rousseau, Hegel, Marx, and Dewey. The former school sees the individual as central and social relationships as a type of a social contract where the individual, using human reason, gives up some rights for the good of the whole or for social justice. The latter tends to see society as central, rather than the individual, and seeks to teach individuals how to behave throughout their life within communities. In this tradition, justice emerges from "communal understandings" (p. 50).

Philosophers and writers coming from a justice perspective frequently deal with issues such as the nature of the universe, the nature of God, fate versus free will, good and evil, and the relationship between human beings and their state.

Competitive theories to that of the ethic of justice are described by Beauchamp and Childress (1984) and Crittenden (1984). In their writings, they spoke of the work of Bentham and Mill and the theories of Act Utilitarianism and Act Deontology. These theories take into account "the consequences of each particular act" (Beauchamp & Childress, 1984, p. 48). Rules serve as guides for Act Utilitarianists and for Act Deontologists, but they can be broken depending on the consequences of a certain act. Those who turn to these forms of ethics are consequentialists, and they practice situational ethics. They may take into consideration concepts of happiness for the greatest number of individuals and even pleasure. They also think about who their actions might hurt. Although acknowledging other theories and their positive aspects in their writings, Beauchamp and

Childress and Crittenden return to the ethic of justic and argue that educational administrators in societies whose governments are committed to certain fundamental principles, such as tolerance, and respect for the fair treatment of all persons, can and should look to laws and public policies for ethical guidance (Beck & Murphy, 1994a, p. 7).

Educators and ethicists from the ethic of justice have had a profound impact on approaches to education and educational leadership. Contemporary ethical writings in education, using the foundational principle of the ethic of justice, include, among others, works by Kohlberg (1981), Beauchamp and Childress (1984), Strike, Haller, and Soltis (1998), Goodlad, Soder, and Sirotnik (1990), and Sergiovanni (1992).

 Kohlberg (1981) argued that, within the liberal tradition, "there is a great concern not only to make schools more just—that is, to provide equality of educational opportunity and to allow freedom of belief—but also to educate so that free and just people emerge from schools" (p. 74). For Kohlberg, "justice is not a rule or set of rules, it is a moral principle . . . a mode of choosing that is universal, a rule of choosing that we want all people to adopt always in all situations" (p. 39). From this perspective, education is not "value free." This model also indicates that schools should teach principles, in particular those of justice, equity, and respect for liberty.

 From the late 1960s through the early 1980s, Kohlberg introduced his "just-community" approach to the schools. In institutions as diverse as Roosevelt High, a comprehensive school in Manhattan, The Bronx High School of Science, and an alternative high school in Cambridge, Massachusetts, students and teachers handled school discipline and sometimes even the running of the school together. In a civil and thoughtful manner, students were taught to deal with problems within the school, turning to rules, rights, and law for guidance (Hersh, Paolitto, & Reimer, 1979).

 Building on Kohlberg's "just community," Sergiovanni (1992) called for moral leadership and, in particular, the principle of justice in the establishment of "virtuous schools." Sergiovanni thought of educational leadership as a stewardship and asked educational administrators to create institutions that are just and beneficent. By beneficence, Sergiovanni meant that there should be deep concern for the welfare of the school as a community, a concept that extends beyond the school walls and into the local community, taking into account not only students, teachers, and administrators, but families as well.

Unlike a number of educators in the field, Sergiovanni's virtuous, rather than effective, schools' concept placed the principle of justice at its center. "Accepting this principle meant that every parent, teacher, student, administrator, and other member of the school community must be treated with the same equality, dignity, and fair play" (pp. 105–106).

The ethic of justice, from either a traditional or contemporary perspective, may take into account a wide variety of issues. Viewing ethical dilemmas from this vantage point, one may ask questions related to the rule of law and the more abstract concepts of fairness, equity, and justice. These may include, but are certainly not limited to, questions related to issues of equity and equality; the fairness of rules, laws, and policies; whether laws are absolute, and if exceptions are to be made, under what circumstances; and the rights of individuals versus the greater good of the community.

Moreover, the ethic of justice frequently serves as a foundation for legal principles and ideals. This important function is evident in laws related to education. In many instances, courts have been reluctant to impose restrictions on school officials, thus allowing them considerable discretion in making important administrative decisions (*Board of Education v. Pico*, 1981). At the same time, court opinions often reflect the values of the education community and society at large (Stefkovich & Guba, 1998). For example, only in recent years have courts upheld the use of metal detectors in schools to screen for weapons (*People v. Dukes*, 1992). In addition, what is legal in some places may be considered illegal in others. For example, corporal punishment (Hyman & Snook, 2000) is still legal in 23 states and strip searching is legal in all but 7 (Stefkovich & O'Brien, 2000). In those states, it is left up to school officials, and the community, whether such practices are to be supported or not. Here, ethical issues such as due process and privacy rights are often balanced against the need for civility and the good of the majority. Finally, what is to be done when a law is wrong, such as earlier Jim Crow laws supporting racial segregation? (Starratt, 1994c). Here, one must turn to ethics to make fair and just decisions. It is also in such instances that the ethic of justice may overlap with other paradigms such as the ethics of critique (Purpel, 1989) and care (Katz, Noddings, & Strike, 1999).

THE ETHIC OF CRITIQUE

Many writers and activists (e.g., Apple, 1988; Bakhtin, 1981; Bowles & Gintis, 1988; Foucault, 1983; Freire, 1970; Giroux, 1994; Greene, 1988; Purpel & Shapiro, 1995) are not convinced by the analytic and rational approach of the justice paradigm. Some of these scholars find a tension between the ethic of justice, rights, and laws, and the concept of democracy. In response, they raise difficult questions by critiquing both the laws themselves and the process used to determine if the laws are just.

Rather than accepting the ethic of those in power, these scholars challenge the status quo by seeking an ethic that will deal with inconsistencies, formulate the hard questions, and debate and challenge the issues. Their intent is to awaken us to our own unstated values and make us realize how frequently our own morals may have been modified and possibly even corrupted over time. Not only do they force us to rethink important concepts such as democracy, but they also ask us to redefine and reframe other concepts such as privilege, power, culture, language, and even justice.

The ethic of critique is based on critical theory, which has, at its heart, an analysis of social class and its inequities. According to Foster (1986), "Critical theorists are scholars who have approached social analysis in an investigative and critical manner and who have conducted investigations of social structure from perspectives originating in a modified Marxian analysis" (p. 71). More recently, critical theorists have turned to the intersection of race and gender as well as social class in their analyses.

An example of the work of critical theorists can be found in their arguments, occuring over many decades, that schools reproduce inequities similar to those in society (Bourdieu, 1977; Lareau, 1987). Tracking, for example, can be seen as one way to make certain that working class children know their place (Oakes, 1993). Generally designed so that students are exposed to different knowledge in each track, schools "[make] decisions about the appropriateness of various topics and skills and, in doing so . . . [limit] . . . sharply what some students would learn" (Oakes, 1993, p. 87). Recognizing this inequity, Carnoy and Levin (1985) pointed to a important contradiction in educational institutions, in that schools also represent the major force in the United States for expanding economic opportunity as well as the extension of democratic rights. Herein lies one of many inconsistencies to be addressed through the ethic of critique.

Along with critical theory, the ethic of critique is also frequently linked to critical pedagogy. Giroux (1991) asked educators to understand that their classrooms are political as well as educational locations and, as such, ethics is not a matter of individual choice or relativism but a "social discourse grounded in struggles that refuse to accept needless human suffering and exploitation." In this respect, the ethic of critique provides "a discourse for expanding basic human rights" (p. 48) and may serve as a vehicle in the struggle against inequality. In this vein, critical theorists are often concerned with making known the voices of those who are silenced, particularly students (Giroux, 1988; Weis & Fine, 1993).

For Giroux (1991), Welch (1991), and other critical educators, the language of critique is central, but discourse alone will not suffice. These scholars are also activists who believe discourse should be a beginning leading to some kind of action—preferably political. For example, Shapiro and Purpel (1993) emphasized empowering people through the discussion of options. Such a dialogue hopefully would provide what Giroux and Aronowitz (1985) called a "language of possibility" that, when applied to educational institutions, might enable them to avoid reproducing the "isms" in society (i.e., classism, racism, sexism, heterosexism).

Turning to educational leadership, in particular, Parker and Shapiro (1993) argued that one way to rectify some wrongs in school and in society would be to give more attention to the analysis of social class in the preparation of principals and superintendents. They believed that social class analysis "is crucial given the growing divisions of wealth and power in the United States, and their impact on inequitable distribution of resources both within and among school districts" (pp. 39–40). Through the critical analysis of social class, there is the possibility that more knowledgeable, moral, and sensitive educational leaders might be prepared.

Capper (1993), in her writings in educational leadership, stressed the need for moral leaders to be concerned with "freedom, equality, and the principles of a democratic society" (p. 14). She provided a nice summary of the roots of, and philosophy supporting, the ethic of critique as it pertains to educational leaders. She spoke of the Frankfurt school in the United States in the 1920s at the New School for Social Research in New York City, in which immigrants tried to make sense of the oppression they had endured in Europe. This school provided not only a Marxist critique but took into account psychology and its effect on the individual. Capper wrote:

> Grounded in the work of the Frankfurt school, critical theorists in educational administration are ultimately concerned with suffering and oppression, and critically reflect on current and historical social inequities. They believe in the imperative of leadership and authority and work toward the empowerment and transformation of followers, while grounding decisions in morals and values . . . (p. 15)

Thus, by demystifying and questioning what is happening in society and in schools, critical theorists may help educators rectify wrongs while identifying key morals and values.

In summary, the ethic of critique, inherent in critical theory, is aimed at awakening educators to inequities in society and, in particular, in the schools. This ethic asks educators to deal with the hard questions regarding social class, race, gender, and other areas of difference, such as: Who makes the laws? Who benefits from the law, rule, or policy? Who has the power? Who are the silenced voices? This approach to ethical dilemmas then asks educators to go beyond questioning and critical analysis to examine and grapple with those possibilities that could enable all children, whatever their social class, race, or gender to have opportunities to grow, learn, and achieve. Such a process should lead to the development of options related to important concepts such as oppression, power, privilege, authority, voice, language, and empowerment.

THE ETHIC OF CARE

Juxtaposing an ethic of care with an ethic of justice, Roland Martin (1993) wrote the following:

> One of the most important findings of contemporary scholarship is that our culture embraces a hierarchy of value that places the productive processes of society and their associated traits above society's reproductive processes and the associated traits of care and nurturance. There is nothing new about this. We are the inheritors of a tradition of Western thought according to which the functions, tasks, and traits associated with females are deemed less valuable than those associated with males. (p. 144)

Some feminist scholars (e.g., Beck, 1994; Belenky, Clinchy, Goldberger, & Tarule, 1986; Gilligan, 1982; Gilligan, Ward, & Taylor, 1988; Marshall, 1995; Noddings, 1984, 1992; Shapiro & Smith-Rosenberg, 1989) have challenged this dominant, and what they consider to be often patriarchal, ethic of justice in our society by turning to the ethic of care for moral decision making. Attention to this ethic can lead to other discussions of concepts such as loyalty, trust, and empowerment. Similar to critical theorists, these feminist scholars emphasize social responsibility, frequently discussed in the light of injustice, as a pivotal concept related to the ethic of care.

In her classic book, *In a Different Voice*, Gilligan (1982) introduced the ethic of care by discussing a definition of justice different from Kohlberg's in the resolution of moral dilemmas (see the ethic of justice section in this chapter). In her research, Gilligan discovered that, unlike the males in Kohlberg's studies who adopted rights and laws for the resolution of moral issues, women and girls frequently turn to another voice, that of care, concern, and connection, in finding answers to their moral dilemmas.

Growing out of the ethic of justice, the ethic of care, as it relates to education, has been described well by Noddings (1992), who created a new educational hierarchy placing "care" at the top when she wrote, "The first job of the schools is to care for our children" (p. xiv). To Noddings, and to a number of other ethicists and educators who advocate the use of the ethic of care, students are at the center of the educational process and need to be nurtured and encouraged, a concept that likely goes against the grain of those attempting to make "achievement" the top priority. Noddings believes that holding on to a competitive edge in achievement means that some children may see themselves merely as pawns in a nation of demanding and uncaring adults. In school buildings that more often resemble large, bureaucratic, physical plants, a major complaint of young people with regard to adults is that "They don't care!" (Comer, 1988). For Noddings, "Caring is the very bedrock of all successful education and . . . contemporary schooling can be revitalized in its light" (p. 27).

Noddings and Gilligan are not alone in believing the ethic of care is essential in education. In relation to the curriculum, Roland Martin (1993) wrote of the three Cs of caring, concern, and connection. Although she does not ask educators to teach "Compassion 101a" or to offer "Objectivity 101a," she does implore them to broaden the curriculum to include the experiences of both sexes, and not just one, and to stop leaving out the ethic of care. For Roland Martin, education is an "integration of reason and emotion, self and other" (p. 144).

Although the ethic of care has been associated with feminists, men and women alike attest to its importance and relevancy. Beck (1994) pointed out that "Caring—as a foundational ethic—addresses concerns and needs as expressed by *many* persons; that it, in a sense, transcends ideological boundaries" (p. 3). Male ethicists and educators, such as Buber (1965) and Sergiovanni (1992), have expressed high regard for this paradigm. These scholars have sought to make education a "human enterprise" (Starratt, 1991, p. 195).

The ethic of care is important not only to scholars but to educational leaders who are often asked to make moral decisions. If the ethic of care is used to resolve dilemmas, then there is a need to revise how educational leaders are prepared. In the past, educational leaders were trained using military and business models. This meant that they were taught about the importance of the hierarchy and the need to follow those at the top and, at the same time, be in command and in charge of subordinates (Guthrie, 1990). They led by developing "rules, policies, standard operating procedures, information systems . . . or a variety of more informal techniques" (Bolman & Deal, 1991, p. 48). These techniques and rules may have worked well when the ethic of justice, rights, and laws was the primary basis for leaders making moral decisions; however, they are inadequate when considering other ethical paradigms, such as the ethic of care, that require leaders to consider multiple voices in the decision-making process.

Beck (1994) stressed that it is essential for educational leaders to move away from a top–down, hierarchical model for making moral and other decisions and, instead, turn to a leadership style that emphasizes relationships and connections. Administrators need to "encourage collaborative efforts between faculty, staff, and students [which would serve] . . . to promote interpersonal interactions, to deemphasize competition, to facilitate a sense of belonging, and to increase individuals' skills as they learn from one another" (p. 85).

When an ethic of care is valued, educational leaders can become what Barth (1990) called, "head learner(s)" (p. 513). Barth meant by that term the making of outstanding leaders and learners who wish to listen to others when facing the need to make important moral decisions. The preparation of these individuals, then, must more heavily focus on the knowledge of cultures and of diversity, with a special emphasis on learning how to listen, observe, and respond to others. For example, Shapiro, Sewell, DuCette, and Myrick (1997), in their study of inner-city youth, identified three different kinds of caring: attention and support; discipline; and "staying on them," or prodding them over time. As to the latter, although prodding students to complete homework might be viewed as nagging, these researchers found the students they studied saw prodding as an indication that someone cared about them.

Thus, the ethic of care offers another perspective and another way to respond to complex moral problems facing educational leaders in their daily work. Viewing ethical dilemmas through this paradigm may prompt questions related to how educators may assist young people in meeting their needs and desires and would reflect solutions that show a concern for others as part of decision making. This ethic asks that individuals consider the consequences of their decisions and actions. It asks them to consider questions such as: Who will benefit from what I decide? Who will be hurt by my actions? What are the long-term effects of a decision I make today? And if I am helped by someone now, what should I do in the future about giving back to this individual or to society in general? This paradigm also asks individuals to grapple with values such as loyalty and trust.

THE ETHIC OF THE PROFESSION

Starratt (1994a) postulated that the ethics of justice, care, and critique are not incompatible, but rather, complementary, the combination of which results in a richer, more complete, ethic. He visualized these ethics as themes, interwoven much like a tapestry:

> An ethical consciousness that is not interpenetrated by each theme can be captured either by sentimentality, by rationalistic simplification, or by social naivete. The blending of each theme encourages a rich human response to the many uncertain ethical situations the school community faces every day, both in the learning tasks as well as in its attempt to govern itself. (p. 57)

We agree with Starratt. But we have also come to believe that, even taken together, the ethics of justice, critique, and care do not provide an adequate picture of the factors that must be taken into consideration as leaders strive to make ethical decisions within the context of educational settings. What is missing—that is, what these paradigms tend to ignore—is a consideration of those moral aspects unique to the profession and the questions that arise as educational leaders become more aware of their own personal and professional codes of ethics. To fill this gap, we add a fourth to the three ethical frameworks described in this chapter, a paradigm of professional ethics.

Although the idea of professional ethics has been with us for some time, identifying the process as we have and presenting it in the form of a paradigm represents a relatively innovative way of conceptualizing this ethic. Because this approach is new—one we have developed through the last 8 years of collaborative research, writing, and teaching ethics—we devote more time to explaining this ethic than was given others.

The remainder of this chapter includes some brief background information on the emergence of professional ethics and the need for a professional ethics paradigm. Following these introductory remarks, we describe our model of professional ethics and how it works. This chapter concludes with a discussion of how the paradigm of professional ethics fits in with the other three ethics of justice, critique, and care.

PROFESSIONAL ETHICS AND THE NEED
FOR A PROFESSIONAL PARADIGM

When discussing ethics in relation to the professionalization of educational leaders, the tendency is to look toward professions such as law, medicine, dentistry, and business, which require their graduate students to take at least one ethics course before graduation as a way of socializing persons into the profession. The field of educational administration has no such ethics requirement. However, the stage has been set for the introduction of ethics.

In recent years, there has been a resurgence of interest in ethics as related to educational decision making. A number of writers in educational administration (Beck, 1994; Beck & Murphy, 1994a, 1994b; Beck, Murphy, & Associates, 1997; Begley & Johansson, 1998; Cambron-McCabe & Foster, 1994; Duke & Grogan, 1997; Mertz, 1997; O'Keefe, 1997; Starratt, 1994a; Willower, 1999) believe it is important to provide prospective administrators with some training in ethics. As Greenfield (1993) pointed out, this preparation could "enable a prospective principal or superintendent to develop the attitudes, beliefs, knowledge, and skills associated with competence in moral reasoning" (p. 285). Stressing the importance for such preparation, Greenfield left us with a warning of sorts:

> A failure to provide the opportunity for school administrators to develop such competence constitutes a failure to serve the children we are obligated to serve as public educators. As a profession, educational administration thus has a moral obligation to train prospective administrators to be able to apply the principles, rules, ideals, and virtues associated with the development of ethical schools. (p. 285)

Recognizing this need, ethics was identified as one of the competencies necessary for school leaders by the Interstate School Leaders Licensure Consortium (ISLLC). This consortium, working under the auspices of the Council of Chief State School Officers and in collaboration with the National Policy Board for Educational Administration (NPBEA), consisted of representatives from 24 states and 9 associations related to the educational administration profession.

In its 1996 document, *Standards for School Leaders,* the ISLLC set forth six standards for the profession. Of these, Standard 5 states that: "A school administrator is an educational leader who promotes the success of all students by acting with integrity, fairness, and in an ethical manner" (ISLLC, 1996, p. 18). To meet this standard, an administrator, among other things, must (a) possess a knowledge and understanding of various ethical frameworks and perspectives on ethics; (b) have a knowledge and understanding of professional codes of ethics; (c) believe in, value, and be committed to bringing ethical principles to the decision-making process; and (d) believe in, value, and be committed to developing a caring school community (ISLLC, 1996, p. 18). This standard, with its requirements, officially recognizes the importance of ethics in the knowledge base for school administrators and, at the same time, deviates from earlier views of professional ethics.

In the past, professional ethics has generally been viewed as a subset of the justice paradigm. This is likely the case because professional ethics is often equated with codes, rules, and principles, all of which fit neatly into traditional concepts of justice (Beauchamp & Childress, 1984). For example, some states have established their own sets of standards. The Pennsylvania Code of Professional Practice and Conduct for Educators (1992) is an 11-point code of conduct that was subsequently enacted into state law. Texas has a similar code of "Ethics, Standards, and Practices" (Texas Administrative Code, 1998) for its educators that, among other things, expects educators to deal justly with students and protect them from "disparagement."

In addition, a number of education-related professional organizations have developed their own professional ethical codes. Defined by Beauchamp and Childress (1984) as "an articulated statement of role morality as seen by members of the profession" (p. 41), some of these ethical codes are relatively new and others are longstanding. Examples of these organizations include, but are certainly not limited to, the American Association of School Administrators, the American Association of University Professors, the American Psychological Association, the Association of School Business Officials, the Association for Supervision and Curriculum Development, and the National Education Association.

However, ethical codes set forth by the states and professional associations tend to be limited in their responsiveness in that they are somewhat removed from the day-to-day personal and professional dilemmas educational leaders face. Nash (1996), in his book on professional ethics for educators and human service professionals, recognized these limitations as he observed his students' lack of interest in such codes:

> What are we to make of this almost universal disparagement of professional codes of ethics? What does the nearly total disregard of professional codes mean? For years, I thought it was something in my delivery that evoked such strong, antagonistic responses. For example, whenever I ask students to bring their codes to class, few knew where to locate them, and most get utterly surly when I make such a request. I understand, now, however, that they do not want to be bothered with what they consider a trivial, irrelevant assignment, because they simply do not see a correlation between learning how to make ethical decisions and appealing to a code of ethics. (p. 95)

On the other hand, professional codes of ethics serve as guideposts for the profession, giving statements about its image and character (Lebacqz, 1985). They embody "the highest moral ideals of the profession," thus "presenting an ideal image of the moral character of both the profession and the professional" (Nash, 1996, p. 96) Seen in this light, standardized codes provide a most valuable function. Thus, the problem lies not so much in the codes themselves, but in the fact that we sometimes expect too much from them with regard to moral decision making (Lebacqz, 1985; Nash, 1996).

Recognizing the importance of standardized codes, the contributions they make, and their limitations, we believe the time has come to view professional ethics from a broader, more inclusive, and more contemporary, perspective. This type of approach is reflected in the ISLLC standards. Focusing on rules, principles, and identification of competencies, these standards are essentially regulatory in nature. At the same time, they acknowledge the importance of knowing different ethical frameworks. And, competence for the profession is assessed through an examination based on a case study approach, that is, an analysis of vignettes asking what factors a school leader should consider in making a decision.

A PARADIGM FOR PROFESSIONAL ETHICS

Our concept of professional ethics as an ethical paradigm includes ethical principles and codes of ethics embodied in the justice paradigm, but is much broader, taking into account other paradigms, as well as professional judgment and professional decision making. We recognize professional ethics as a dynamic process requiring that administrators develop their own personal and professional codes.

We believe this process is important, and like Nash, observed a dissonance between students' own codes and those set forth by states or professional groups. For the most part, our students were not aware of these codes or, if they were, such formalized professional codes had little impact on them; most found it more valuable to create their own codes. As one of our students, a department chair, pointed out after his involvement in this process:

> Surprisingly to me, I even enjoyed doing the personal and professional ethics statements. I have been in union meetings where professional ethical codes were discussed. They were so bland and general as to be meaningless. Doing these statements forced me to think about what I do and how I live whereas the previous discussions did not. It was a very positive experience. I also subscribe to the notion that [standardized] professional ethical codes are of limited value. I look to myself to determine what decisions I can live with. Outside attempts at control have little impact on me and what I do.

Through our work, we have come to believe educational leaders should be given the opportunity to take the time to develop their own personal codes of ethics based on life stories and critical incidents and their own professional codes based on the experiences and expectations of their working lives as well as a consideration of their personal codes.

Underlying such a process is an understanding of oneself as well as others. These understandings necessitate that administrators reflect upon concepts such as what they perceive to be right or wrong and good or bad, who they are as professionals and as human beings, how they make decisions, and why they make the decisions they do. This process recognizes that preparing students to live and work in the 21st century requires very special administrators who have grappled with their own personal and professional codes of ethics and have reflected on diverse forms of ethics, taking into account the differing backgrounds of the students enrolled in U.S. schools today.

By grappling, we mean that these educational leaders have struggled over issues of justice, critique, and care related to the education of children and youth, and through this process, have gained a sense of who they are and what they believe personally and professionally. It means coming to grips with clashes that may arise among ethical codes and making ethical decisions in light of their best professional judgment, a judgment that places the best interests of the student at the center of all ethical decision making.

, Thus, actions by school officials are likely to be strongly influenced by personal values (Begley & Johansson, 1998; Willower & Lacata, 1997), and personal codes of ethics build on these values and experiences (Shapiro & Stefkovich, 1997, 1998). As many of our students found, it is not always easy to separate professional from personal ethical codes. The observations of this superintendent of a large rural district aptly sums up our own experiences and the sentiments of many of our practitioner-students:

> A professional ethical code cannot be established without linkage and reference to one's personal code of ethics and thereby acknowledges such influencing factors. In retrospect, and as a result of . . . [developing my own ethical codes], I can see the influence professional responsibilities have upon my personal values, priorities, and behavior. It seems there is an unmistakable "co-influence" of the two codes. One cannot be completely independent of the other. (Shapiro & Stefkovich, 1998, p. 137)

Other factors that play into the development of professional codes include consideration of community standards, including both the professional community and the community in which the leader works; formal codes of ethics established by professional associations; and written standards of the profession (ISLLC).

As educational leaders develop their professional (and personal) codes, they consider various ethical models, either focusing on specific paradigms or, optimally, integrating the ethics of justice, care, and critique. This filtering process provides the basis for professional judgments and professional ethical decision making; it may also result in clashes among codes.

Through our work, we have identified four possible clashes, three of which have been discussed earlier (Shapiro & Stefkovich, 1998). First, there may be clashes between an individual's personal and professional codes of ethics. Second, there may be clashes within professional codes. This may occur when an individual's personal ethical code conflicts with an ethical code set forth by the profession or when the individual has been prepared in two or more professions. Codes of one profession may be different from another. Hence, a code that serves an individual well in one career may not in another. Third, there may be clashes of professional codes among educational leaders; what one administrator sees as ethical, another may not. Fourth, there may be clashes between a leader's personal and professional code of ethics and custom and practices set forth by the community (i.e., either the professional community, the school community, or the community where the educational leader works). For example, a number of our students noted that some behavior that may be considered unethical in one community might in another community merely be seen as a matter of personal preference.

To resolve these conflicts, we harken back to Greenfield's earlier (1993) quote that grounded the "moral dimension" for the preparation of school administrators in the needs of children. Greenfield contended that schools, particularly public schools, should be the central sites for "preparing children to assume the roles and responsibilities of citizenship in a democratic society" (p. 268).

Not all those who write about the importance of the study of ethics in educational administration discuss the needs of children; however, this focus on students is clearly consistent with the backbone of our profession. Other professions often have one basic principle driving the profession. In medicine, it is "First, do no harm." In law, it is the assertion that all clients deserve "zealous representation." In educational administration, we believe that if there is a moral imperative for the profession, it is to serve the "best interests of the student." Consequently, this ideal must lie at the heart of any professional paradigm for educational leaders.

This focus is reflected in most professional association codes. For example, the American Association of School Administrators' *Statement of Ethics for School Administrators* (American Association of School Administrators, 1981) begins with the assertion: "An educational administrator's professional behavior *must conform to an ethical code*" and has as its first tenet this statement: "The educational administrator . . . makes the *well-being of students* the *fundamental value* of all decision making and actions" [italics added]. It is in concert with Noddings' (1992) ethic of care, which places students at the top of the educational hierarchy, and is reflective of the concerns of many critical theorists who see students' voices as silenced (Giroux, 1988; Weis & Fine, 1993). And serving the best interests of the student is consistent with the ISLLC's standards for the profession, each of which begins with the words: "A school administrator is an educational leader who *promotes the success of all students* by . . ." (ISLLC, 1996, italics added).

Frequent confrontations with moral dilemmas become even more complex as dilemmas increasingly involve a variety of student populations, parents, and communities comprising diversity in broad terms that extend well beyond categories of race and ethnicity. In this respect, differences encompassing cultural categories of race and ethnicity, religion, social class, gender, disability, and sexual orientation as well as individual differences that may take into account learning styles, exceptionalities, and age often cannot be ignored (Banks & Banks, 1993; Cushner, McClelland, & Safford, 1992; Gollnick & Chinn, 1994; Shapiro, Sewell, & DuCette, 1995; Sleeter & Grant, 1988).

In sum, we have described a paradigm for the profession that expects its leaders to formulate and examine their own professional codes of ethics in light of individual personal codes of ethics, as well as standards set forth by the profession, and then calls on them to place students at the center of the ethical decision-making process. As such, the professional paradigm we are proposing is dynamic—not static—and multidimensional, recognizing the complexities of being an educational leader in today's society. (See Fig. 2.1 for a visual representation of this model.)

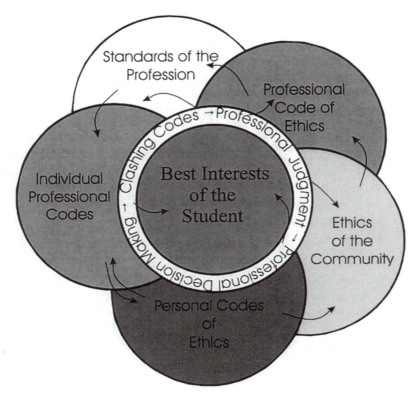

FIG. 2.1. Diagrammatic representation of the ethic of the profession. The circles indicate major factors that converge to create the professional paradigm. The circles shown are: standards of the profession, professional code of ethics, ethics of the community, personal codes of ethics, individual professional codes, and best interests of the student. Other factors also play a part in the professional paradigm. They are found surrounding the best interests of the student circle and include: clashing codes, professional judgment, and professional decision making. The arrows indicate the various ways the factors interact and overlap with each other.

Thus, taking all these factors into consideration, this ethic of the profession would ask questions related to justice, critique, and care posed by the other ethical paradigms, but would go beyond these questions to ask what the profession would expect and what is in the best interests of the students taking into account the fact that they may represent highly diverse populations.

II

A MULTIPARADIGM
APPROACH TO ANALYZING
PARADOXICAL DILEMMAS

The next five chapters present ethical dilemmas that lend themselves to analysis through a multiparadigm approach. They highlight inherent inconsistencies existing within education in particular, and our communities in general, that tend to give rise to dilemmas. Thus, we have framed each chapter as a paradox, and the cases included illustrate the tensions that surround the concept. The paradoxes highlighted are individual rights versus community standards; the traditional curriculum versus the hidden curriculum; personal codes versus professional codes; the American melting pot versus the Chinese hot pot; and equality versus equity.

Purpel (1989), in describing the moral and spiritual crisis in contemporary education, turned to paradoxes to bring out many current problems and tensions. We agree with him that many of today's strains and stresses have occurred because of the contradictions that exist in our society. When these paradoxes are brought to the reader's attention, through the discussion of real-life dilemmas, we hope that they will not only lead to stimulating conversations, but that they will also encourage reflection and guidance for wise decision making in the future.

Because many of the dilemmas are based on true experiences, there has been a genuine effort to make certain anonymity and confidentiality have been maintained. The cases are meant to be used in educational administration classes and in other courses related to education or leadership in general. They are intended to make certain that students and other readers are exposed to differing paradigms and diverse voices—of justice, rights, and law; care, concern, and connectedness; critique and possibility; and professionalism. They also reflect the diversity of students and of communities in a complex era.

These cases focus on persons holding a variety of positions in school systems. In constructing the scenarios, we purposely tried to balance the gender, race, ethnicity, and age of both the persons confronting the dilemmas and the persons with whom they had to deal. In this respect, we gave these persons names that would reflect this diversity. We were very conscious of the risks in not giving everyone Anglo-sounding names, as is the usual practice in case studies, and consciously tried to avoid reinforcing or adapting stereotypes. However, we feel that in view of our diverse, multicultural school communities, this was the most appropriate approach. We apologize in advance for any stereotyping that may have occurred inadvertently.

Before we turn to the cases in the next few chapters, we provide a brief illustration of how ethical dilemmas may be viewed through a multiparadigm lens. We turn to a dilemma that we developed and used toward the beginning of our course called *The School Uniform Case*. When we first discussed this case, we raised issues associated with the ethic of justice dealing with the legal ramifications of school uniforms. Although our students understood the concepts associated with the justice paradigm and learned much from this analysis, they also seemed frustrated and we began to think that the discussion was incomplete. Instinctively, we and our students began to bring in other analyses related to the ethics of care, critique, and the profession. These paradigms tended to complement the justice perspective and no longer limited the discussion.

It was by reflecting on this process, and other subsequent similar situations, that we came to realize dilemmas are best viewed in a multidimensional, or kaleidoscopic fashion, as through a series of lenses. What follows is a brief synopsis of *The School Uniform Case*, some of the issues presented in this dilemma, and some suggestions for analysis using four paradigms. This is not meant to be a complete analysis of the case, as such an endeavor would take up more time and space than we feel is necessary for the intent of this introduction. Instead, we use this case and the suggested approaches only as an illustration as to how to reflect upon an ethical dilemma through the use of multiple paradigms.

The School Uniform Case is about a poor, inner-city teenager named Tom, who came to school wearing a new pair of tennis shoes. The shoes were expensive and he said that he had saved 3 weeks of his salary from his after-school job to pay for them. Tom was extremely proud of his shoes and showed them off to everyone. The next day, the school was in an uproar when the news came that Tom had been killed. Only a few days later, a 17-year-old classmate of Tom's was seen walking in a new pair of tennis shoes identical to those Tom had worn.

Prior to the murder, the school's principal, Dr. Smith, had suffered little irritations regarding students' dress. She became tired of overhearing students complaining that they had nothing new to wear, and she was annoyed at their tardiness due to taking hours to dress for school. But the killing of a student only indicated how severe the problem really had become. There were many issues related to this terrible situation, but, in an effort to do something soon, Dr. Smith decided to consider a disarmingly simple solution for dealing with the problem of envy over other students' possessions. She decided to take seriously the idea of requiring that each student wear a school uniform.

Although this solution sounded simple and appropriate to Dr. Smith, we recommend that she pause and reflect on this dilemma, taking into account four paradigms or lenses before deciding that school uniforms are the answer. If, for example, Dr. Smith analyzed the case using the ethic of justice, she would have to look closely at laws, rules, and principles regarding dress codes. These reflections have to take into account the laws regarding public schools and students' rights. Dr. Smith would need to consider the First Amendment and the free speech clause within it. A dress code, it could be argued, would come under symbolic free speech. However, despite the law, students might be regulated, particularly if they were indecent or immodest in dress or disrupted the learning process in some way. Under the ethic of justice, then, Dr. Smith might ask the following: In a public school, do students have a right to choose what they want to wear? How far does this right extend or are there any limits on their dress?

Turning to the ethic of care, it is clear that Dr. Smith is concerned about her students' safety. She believes that school uniforms would be a great equalizer and would protect individual students from future dangers caused by others' envy of their clothes. Additionally, aware of the poverty in her area, she cares about her students' finances. School uniforms would no doubt be a great savings for her students and their families. In this regard, using the lens of care and concern, some questions she could raise for reflection and discussion include: Shouldn't the school uniform be required because it will serve as an equalizer and, hence, help to make students safe? Won't the requirement of a school uniform assist students in a poverty area who currently pay too much money for designer clothes and jewelry?

If Dr. Smith turns to the ethic of critique, questions of a broader nature could be asked, such as: What kind of system encourages young people to compete with each other over clothes and fosters envy to such a degree that a young person would kill over what another wears? How can this system be made better, enabling students to focus on learning rather than on spending money and effort on clothes and jewelry?

Finally, if Dr. Smith turns to the professional ethical paradigm, she might consider all these questions and then go beyond them to determine if there were inconsistencies. One way to accomplish this would be by asking: What would the profession expect her to do? And what solutions are in the best interests of the students? Still keeping in mind the professional paradigm, she might also ask this key question: Is it in the best interest of students to require that they be dressed in school uniforms?

Thus, what at the outset looks like a simple solution to a disturbing problem becomes something quite different and far more complex. This type of questioning, using four different paradigms, hopefully would provide Dr. Smith with in-depth and detailed knowledge and sensitivities regarding school uniforms. Although it might take longer than she orginally intended to reach a decision, what Dr. Smith decided to do would no doubt be wiser and more informed because of the different perspectives and varied approaches she had used.

Now let us turn to chapter 3, which contains the first of the paradoxes and the cases that illustrate some of the tensions as they relate to schooling. This paradox centers around individual rights versus community standards.

3

Individual Rights Versus Community Standards

G. Michaele O'Brien
Kimberly D. Callahan
John A. Schlegel
Loree P. Guthrie

> *In this chapter, dilemmas are presented that focus on community standards. Frequently, in these cases, the standards of the community are pitted against individual rights. In reading and discussing the dilemmas, we expect that the reader must begin to grapple with the differing views of ethics in demographically shifting communities.*

One of the paradoxes American society faces is that of individual rights versus community standards. This dichotomy emanates from individuals' desire to be unique, independent, and hold a strong self-identity. Yet, at the same time, people seek interdependence by developing strong human and symbolic relationships (Purpel, 1989). This need for a group identity compels communities to develop their own identities, ultimately creating community standards. However, moral dilemmas may arise when community standards conflict with individual rights.

The balance between the needs of both the individual and the greater community goes back to the foundations of the American republic. It is natural that the education of our nation's students has always fueled this debate. The "special position of trust and responsibility" teachers hold, given their proximity to youth, makes the situation unique (DeMitchell, 1993, p. 217). Educational administrators are the natural buffer of this paradox as it manifests itself especially in the public school setting. Specifically, the view of the teacher as role model for students based on an ethical foundation of different communities contrasts with the principle of individual rights. This tension between the community and individual rights must be faced frequently by those administrators working at the very heart of the debate. Since the move away from the common school to the establishment of the school system and profession of teaching, administrators have had to balance community ethics and teacher privacy rights.

Early schooling in America was characterized by teacher conduct as a matter of public concern (Tyack, 1974). Throughout the first half of the 19th century, schools fell largely under local community control (DeMitchell, 1993). As such, most details of teachers' lives were placed under the control and scrutiny of local community members. Matters such as marital status, dress, and living arrangements were often direct conditions of employment (Hoffman, 1981; Tyack, 1974). However, as reformers after 1850 began to make progress toward the establishment of bureaucratized school systems, the "rise of professionalism" began to "counterbalance community control" (DeMitchell, 1993, p. 217). Certainly, teachers were still accountable to the public for life outside of the classroom. However, the rise of a school bureaucracy often made the scrutiny less intense. The picture of the teacher as role model began to be joined by a vision of the teacher as private individual.

The following discussion took place during proceedings of the Supreme Court of Pennsylvania in 1993:

> [I]mmorality is not essentially confined to deviation from sex morality; it may be such a course of action as offends the morals of the community and is a bad example to the youth whose ideals a teacher is supposed to foster and to elevate. . . . It has always been the recognized duty of the teacher to conduct himself in such a way as to command the respect and good will of the community, though one result of the choice of a teacher's vocation may be to deprive him of the same freedom of action enjoyed by persons in other vocations. (DeMitchell, 1993, p. 221)

Despite the shift away from direct community control, it was not until the 1960s and 1970s that there was any significant movement toward acceptance of greater personal freedom for teachers. Yet, in many cases, selection and retention of teachers continued to remain intertwined based on community values and expectations. Even into the latter half of the 20th century, dismissal of teachers for conduct outside of school was practiced by various communities (*McBroom v. Board of Education*, 1986).

The paradox between community control and individual rights continues to thrive. There has been a strong "move away from the community's ability to police the private lives of teachers. Along with the courts, many school administrators and boards of education are looking for a direct relationship between teacher action and adverse effect on students, and/or school or both, when considering any action against a teacher for personal conduct" (*Morrison v. Board of Education*, 1969). Although court cases may illuminate the issues surrounding the dispute between teacher as exemplar and teacher as private citizen, administrators must continue to fill a unique role. They frequently must deal with the move to objectify criteria that may be used to balance the community view of teachers as role model and the idea of teacher as professional.

In this chapter, individual rights and personal liberties are juxtaposed against the standards of the community. The chapter provides a forum for the discussion of moral absolutism and theories of consequentialism and nonconsequentialism (as explained in chapter 1). Important questions to be asked include: Are there values and moral standards that are absolute or fixed? Do the ends ever justify the means? In considering these questions, this chapter examines the changing face of ethics in different communities.

The three ethical dilemmas examined in this chapter are: "The Adult Fantasy Center," "Artificial Insemination," and "The Trouble with 'Daddy's Roomate'."

In "The Adult Fantasy Center," a male teacher's job is in jeopardy because his principal has found out that he moonlights as a sex shop manager. The principal knows that the parents in her community would find this teacher's other job objectionable.

In "Artificial Insemination," an unmarried teacher in her late 30s confides to her friend, the district's personnel director, that she wants to be artificially inseminated. In this small, rural community that is largely Christian fundamentalist, the personnel director is concerned about the teacher's personal plan as well as the community's reactions to it.

"The Trouble with 'Daddy's Roomate'" shows the difficulties with community values. However, in this case, one might ask: Is there a consensus regarding values within a community? In this dilemma, a parent complains about a book assigned in school that deals with sexual orientation and other sensitive issues.

In all of these cases, the educational administrator must attempt to view each dilemma from the vantage point of the individual and from that of the community, asking questions such as: When do community standards take precedence over individual rights and liberties? Is the ethical character of educators set at a higher level than those of other citizens in the community? Does the community have a right to place educators at a higher ethical level than its other citizens? Should the community have input into matters regarding school employees' individual liberties? These questions are at the heart of the case studies in this chapter.

THE ADULT FANTASY CENTER

Dr. Angela DiNardo was exhausted. Friday afternoons were always filled with emergencies that could never wait until Monday. During her 3 years as assistant principal at Madison High School, Angela could not remember the last time she left her office before 5 p.m. Angela looked for her "homework folder" to place in her briefcase. This afternoon she would try to leave around 4 p.m. Her thoughts were interrupted when her secretary entered with a typed observation report to be signed.

This particular observation report was one that Dr. DiNardo enjoyed completing because it described and evaluated a lesson taught by Ted Tressler. Ted appeared to be the consummate professional. His students respected him and were extremely attentive in class. He constantly introduced innovative teaching methods into the health and physical education curriculum. The applied concepts taught in the classroom were transferred to real-life situations, motivating the students to do well in health class. The health teacher led his department in a concerted effort to modify teaching styles to increase student learning. For several of Mr. Tressler's students, it was an unhappy time when the bell rang indicating the end of class. This was evident by the sad looks on their faces and the approach of some of them to Mr. Tressler's desk to schedule additional time for tutoring. Interestingly enough, the majority of those students were female.

The administration had approached Ted several times during his 5 years at Madison, asking him to coach various teams throughout the seasons. Angela always questioned why he declined such opportunities, which could prove to be beneficial if he chose to apply for the athletic director's position, the next logical career step for him. Although she was anxious to mentor her faculty, in this case Angela had never actually approached Ted about his unwillingness to coach. She assumed his family responsibilities or his frequent tutoring sessions failed to allow him extra time in his schedule to coach. This was unfortunate, Angela thought.

The clock said 4:05 p.m. Dr. DiNardo knew her secretary expected her to have left 5 minutes ago and would not want to wait a minute longer to photocopy the observation report. Reviewing her suggestions for improvement, Angela recalled an incident that occurred toward the end of the class period she had observed. A female student had asked Mr. Tressler a legitimate question dealing with the curriculum. Immediately following his response, he added an unnecessary compliment that bordered on what Angela construed to be sexual harassment. The class period had gone so well and had been conducted in such a professional manner that she felt, at that time, the phrase was reflective of the teacher's expressive nature and dismissed any thoughts of mentioning this in written form. She hoped this was a good decision and one that her superintendent would have approved. Dr. DiNardo signed the observation report with little hesitation and handed it to her secretary. Happy Friday!

Angela always tried to plan her weekends so that her activities provided a balance between work and relaxation time. She was pleased that tonight was a 40th birthday party for a long-time high school friend. It sounded as if it would be fun because Angela and her husband were told that they had to bring an interesting "gag" gift to get in the door, something that would help the friend cope with an anticipated "midlife crisis."

The party was a surprise and would begin promptly at 7 p.m. Angela's husband was away on business and would not be back until just before the party, so it was left up to her, with less than 2 hours to spare, to purchase a gift, shower, and dress. Where could she go for a quick shopping excursion for a "gag" gift? Just then, Angela passed The Adult Fantasy Center. "Why not?" she thought. Something really silly from a place like that might just work. After all, her friend was a bit outrageous.

The Adult Fantasy Center was an establishment deemed by many to be offensive, presenting an eyesore to those living in the upscale Madison community. The store was situated just across the border between a squalid borough and the wealthy township of Madison. In fact, when it first opened, The Adult Fantasy Center had been rumored to have in the back of the store a red velvet curtain separating the legal business from one of unlawful endeavors. Several Madison community members had exhausted all efforts protesting the establishment, fearing that the escort service advertised was really a cover for an illegal prostitution ring. However, they had not succeeded because the store was not within their borders and nothing illegal had developed. Angela had no time to spare. Assuming she would not run into anyone she knew, Angela began her shopping expedition.

Ted Tressler knew that he was about 30 minutes late to work that night. Friday nights were always busy. Steve would just have to understand. After all, on Wednesday night Ted had closed the store at 2 a.m. Teaching all day Thursday was difficult, but he had somehow coped. Who would have known how lucrative the "adult business" would be? Ted sighed. He initially agreed only to financially support Steve Wilkins in his business venture and serve as a silent partner. Steve really needed help from his old college roommate and, after all, if Ted could make as much money as Steve claimed possible, how could he resist investing his inheritance from his grandmother's will?

Ted's wife knew the amount of money that the business was accruing and was pleasantly surprised herself. Putting three children through college was extremely expensive. The Adult Fantasy Center had been very busy lately, despite the strong opposition felt throughout the neighboring community. Fortunately, no one in Madison High School or that district was aware of Ted's business venture. Not that he had anything to hide; from Ted's perspective, the business was entirely legal. But conservative society members might feel that his part ownership of an adult center was indecorous, recognizing his position as a public school role model. Ted and his wife preferred that his second profession be kept a secret.

Ted's thoughts stopped as he entered the parking lot of the store. The lot was not filled. This was a relief. As he entered, he noticed that the shipment of new CD-Roms, which arrived yesterday afternoon, had not been shelved. He would have to speak to the new employee just hired last week and give better directions. He laughed to himself, wondering if a course at Madison High should be implemented stressing job responsibilities. The new employee had been graduated from Madison 4 years ago. The rest of the store looked ready to go for the upcoming weekend. The videos were in place and other paraphernalia was restocked. Ted decided to look for Steve, whom he had somehow missed seeing all week. Ted hoped that Steve's disappearance was not a hint of what might happen in the future. From the initial phases of this business venture, it was made clear that Steve and Ted were partners, but Ted felt as though he already had been doing more than his share.

I will only be a minute, Angela told herself. As she entered the store, she glanced around at the other customers and then at the various merchandise. Not seeing any signs for a gift section, she began perusing what seemed like infinite numbers of sexual paraphernalia. Angela was shopping with such strict focus and intent, wanting to understand the functions of the gadgets she was looking at and anxious to achieve her mission as soon as possible, that she almost did not hear the loud arguments coming from the back of the store. As a result of her broken concentration, Angela looked up, only to see Ted Tressler coming through the red velvet curtain. He turned and clearly recognized Angela. The embarrassment on both sides was overwhelming. Putting the merchandise back on the shelf, she said, "Hello, Ted. What are you doing here?"

Questions for Discussion

1. Are teachers role models for young people? For their students? Why or why not? If teachers are role models, is it acceptable for a teacher to be part owner of an adult center?

2. Is a teacher's second profession anyone's concern, other than his or her own?

3. If the community became aware of Mr. Tressler's second profession, might it believe this profession would have an effect on his performance in the classroom? Would the students think of Mr. Tressler differently and view him in an entirely new light if they knew about his other job?

4. The consequentialist theory "relies solely on consequences to judge the morality of an action" (Strike, Haller, & Soltis, 1988, p. 19). Decisions must be made only to result in the greatest happiness for the greatest number, producing maximum benefits for all. What would the outcome of this case be if Dr. DiNardo subscribed to this theory?

5. A nonconsequentialist theory does not hold consequences to be crucial to the decision being made. Instead, deontologists treat people as ends rather than means and respect their freedom of choice. How would Dr. DiNardo handle this situation if she preferred the nonconsequentialist approach?

6. What about Dr. DiNardo's role in finding out about Mr. Tressler's second profession? How could she explain her own behavior with regard to shopping at the Adult Fantasy Center if those in power found out? How might Dr. DiNardo's behavior affect her standing in the local community? Is an administrator exempt from the same kind of scrutiny as teachers?

7. Does the fact that Mr. Tressler has his own children to send to college affect the morality of his decision? Would your answer be different if it were clear that working in the Adult Fantasy Center was the only way that Mr. Tressler could make enough money to support his family? To educate his children?

8. Could Mr. Tressler's decision to take on this particular job be justified when one considers that his job as a teacher is valued so little by society that he is unable to earn enough from it to support his family? To educate his children?

9. What should Dr. DiNardo do? What would be in the best interests of the students? Would you see this decision differently if the principal were male? If Ted Tressler were female?

ARTIFICIAL INSEMINATION

Sally Fabian is a competent senior high school art teacher with 10 years of teaching experience. She is an advisor to the high school cheerleading squad and volunteers her time to serve on a number of school curriculum committees. She is single and during the past year had shared with the district's personnel director the fact that she wanted to be artificially inseminated. Her goal was to parent a child of her own whom she intended to raise as a single mother.

Having thought about being a single parent for several years, Ms. Fabian went through the required process of counseling for a year. Although she did not maintain a steady relationship with any man, she had dated during her 10 years as a teacher at North High. Sally had been raised in New York City. She chose to attend a small rural college located about 30 miles from North High School. She decided on this particular college because of its excellent academic reputation as well as the advice from one of her high school teachers. During her 4 years in college, Sally fell in love with the area. She felt fortunate when she was hired as a teacher at North High. Sally was a resident of the school district where she taught. In fact, she had recently bought a house directly across from the high school.

Sally's political views could be labeled moderate. She is a registered independent voter. During college she had done an internship in the local Planned Parenthood Clinic. The community that the school district serves is conservative with a small, but unified, group of fundamentalist Christians who are politically active and vitally interested in educational matters. The community as a whole has a rich German heritage along with some traces of ethnic and racial diversity.

As the ethnic and racial composition of the community diversified, the community needed to address the accusation that the lifelong residents are prejudiced and refuse to include all community residents in the mainstream of town life. The increase in the diversity of the community can be attributed partly to the increase in advertisement in larger urban settings for people to move into the area to take advantage of low-income housing. This was a venture taken on by several local businessmen who sought to make substantial financial gains.

Last year, to meet the demands of this growing, rapidly changing, and often contentious population, the school board approved a new administrative position, director of personnel and community relations. John Edwards was the individual selected to fill this slot. All of Mr. Edwards' teaching experience came from his tenure at a large urban high school where he had taught social studies. Directly before assuming this new position, he had been principal at North High, where he had established himself as an effective leader who worked well with students, teachers, and the community.

Mr. Edwards was committed to school reform and believed all stakeholders ought to be able to provide input into the change process. As principal, Mr. Edwards had formed an advocacy group of stakeholders to engage in the change process. He was respected by the community, and he sought to conduct himself in a manner that was consistent with community values. Consequently, change did not come about in an abrupt fashion.

Mr. Edwards is friendly with Sally Fabian and knew of her dream, but he had wondered if she were really serious about it. Now, today, Sally had stopped by Mr. Edwards' office to tell him the "good news." She had decided to go forth with the procedure. Mr. Edwards is in a quandary as to how to handle this delicate situation. As an educational leader in this district, he is concerned with the growing number of teen pregnancies, especially at North High. Nevertheless, he believes teachers are entitled to a private life outside of school, and what one does on one's own time is no business of anyone so long as it does not harm others.

Mr. Edwards is concerned that the community will be enraged if Ms. Fabian goes through with her plan. Furthermore, he is uneasy about his own stake in this case if it became known that he had done nothing to prevent her from pursuing her goal. The question that Mr. Edwards must answer is whether he should, or even if he has the right to, discuss this issue with Ms. Fabian. Moreover, if Mr. Edwards discusses his concerns with Ms. Fabian, should the discussion be an exchange of ideas or should Mr. Edwards demand that she not follow through with her plan? And, does he have an obligation to inform the superintendent or the new principal at North High, both of whom are very conservative in their outlook?

Questions for Discussion

1. Does Mr. Edwards have a right to intercede in Ms. Fabian's decision to have a child as an unmarried person? If so, what are the possible approaches he might take? What is his best course of action?

2. Does the community have a right to challenge Sally's decision to have a child? To ask that she lose her job if she carries forth her plan? In this case, who is the community and do you think they are all speaking in one voice?

3. Would Ms. Fabian be a poor teacher simply because she had a baby out of wedlock?

4. Inasmuch as Sally is not required to discuss her private life at school, is there any reason that the students would be affected by her actions? Is Sally setting a poor example for her students? Why or why not? Does it make a difference that Sally is an adult and her students are minors? Does it make a difference that Sally is going to be artificially inseminated? Would you see the situation differ-

ently if Sally had a long-term live-in relationship with a man and decided to get pregnant? If she became pregnant through the usual means but didn't know who the father of her child was?

THE TROUBLE WITH "DADDY'S ROOMMATE"

Did anyone ever say the job was going to be easy? No, of course not, but one hoped the positives would outweigh the negatives. That, however, did not seem to be the case today.

Wedgewood High School's principal, Mary Evans, a former English teacher (and perhaps more comfortable in that role) had just received a briefing regarding the recent action of her new assistant principal, Howard Brill. Brill's action was precipitated by a problem brought to his attention by Mr. Robert Press, a very irate parent.

The parent of a special education child in the school, Mr. Press was incensed that his son was being exposed to some "trash about queers" presented by his teacher that day in class. Mr. Press complained his son had come home with the news that another English class was reading the children's book *Daddy's Roommate*. This book is about a gay parent and his relationship with a male friend. The assistant principal promised Mr. Press that he would immediately get to the bottom of the situation and see it was righted. Mr. Brill's first call was upstairs to the English Department, at which time he demanded that the chairperson inform him of what was going on.

She told him that Elizabeth Bennett, a senior English teacher who had been with the school district for 15 years and who had an excellent reputation, decided to do a unit on minority groups and the prejudices encountered by them. Censorship was an additional topic in this unit. To let her class know that there are many minority groups that experience prejudice and censorship, Ms. Bennett assigned a variety of literary works such as *The Diary of Anne Frank, Animal Farm, Inherit the Wind*, and finally the two children's books *Little Black Sambo* and *Daddy's Roommate*. Although each member of the class had a copy of all the classics, they did not have copies of the two children's books. These books were presented in class for discussion.

What happened on the day in question was entirely beyond Ms. Bennett's control. Basil Howard, another English teacher (who is considered poor, at best, by his colleagues) saw the book *Daddy's Roommate* on Ms. Bennett's desk and took it. Without stopping to ask why such a book was in a senior-level English class, Howard, enraged, went to his class where he presented the book to his students, making satirical and angry comments about the content of the book. As the remarks became louder, the special education teacher, Paul Jenkins, came by and joined in the book-bashing session. Jenkins then took the book to his special education class and presented it with less than favorable comments; hence, the angry phone call to the assistant principal.

Complaints of parents are taken very seriously by the district's central office administration, and past practice has been to accede to the parents' wishes. Thus, Mr. Brill, the new assistant principal, thought he was taking appropriate action when he banned both *Little Black Sambo* and *Daddy's Roommate* from the curriculum. However, he was hardly prepared for the passionate reaction of Ms. Bennett, who went directly to the principal and stated that Mr. Brill had violated her academic freedom and demanded that the books in question be reinstated.

Principal Evans knew she needed to act quickly before the incident escalated further. She also knew her action had to be fair to all concerned. To complicate matters further, Mary Evans had very strong convictions concerning censorship. She could not ignore these convictions now.

Questions for Discussion

1. Which persons will be affected by Mary Evans' decision? What would each of these persons like to see done? Is there a solution to this problem that would be fair and just to all those concerned? If so, what is it?

2. Is it important to teach students about prejudice and censorship? Why? Is there anything morally wrong with the way Elizabeth Bennett is presenting this issue? Why or why not? Is Principal Evans' decision regarding the book censorship a moral decision? Why or why not?

3. How do you personally feel about censorship? Are your convictions different when applied to a school setting? Why or why not? Do school personnel have a moral obligation to expose students to a multiplicity of ideas? To protect students from knowing about certain issues? Explain your answers.

4. What would you do if you were in Principal Evans' place? Would your decision be different if the issue were strictly political rather than one dealing with sex or sexual orientation?

4

Traditional Curriculum Versus Hidden Curriculum

Leon D. Poeske
Spencer S. Stober
James C. Dyson
Lynn A. Cheddar

This chapter moves instructional issues beyond the classroom and even the school. It asks educators to consider their own values in relation to their curricular selections and hopefully makes them aware of some unintended outcomes for their students, the school, and the community regarding what they choose to teach or what they must teach.

In American education today, one of the paradoxes that exists has to do with the curriculum. Some writers (e.g., Bennett, 1989; Bloom, 1987; Hirsch, 1987; Ravitch & Finn, 1987) have emphasized the necessity to keep the traditional curriculum of U.S. schools in place. By this, they mean holding on to the classical canon and maintaining meanings and knowledge that have stood the test of time. Above all, these authors focus on the need for shared values and a communal culture.

At the same time, other writers (e.g., Anyon, 1980; Apple, 1988; Fine, 1991; Giroux, 1992; Greene, 1978) have stressed the importance of critiquing the traditional curriculum. In their critiques, these scholars have exposed the hidden curriculum of domination (Purpel & Shapiro, 1995). They have drawn people's attention to traditional education that tends to reproduce the inequalities within society. This curriculum of domination teaches many young people to be competitive, individualistic, and authoritarian. It also labels and places a number of students on educational tracks that lead to limited success in adult life.

Although traditionalists may make the claim that their curriculum is value-free and apolitical, this assumption can be challenged. Consistently schools have conveyed the message of "possessive individualism" and "meritocracy." Implicit in the traditional curriculum is the notion that if one doesn't succeed, it is one's own fault. Also implicit is the concept that those who are not middle-class, White, male, and Eurocentric are frequently considered to be "others" (i.e., different sex, race, ethnicity, sexual orientation, and culture).

Critical theorists who have exposed the hidden curriculum have done so through the use of inquiry. They have asked specific questions such as: What should be taught about Christopher Columbus? How should the "discovery" of America be presented to students? What are the "facts" and how should they be explored by students? These critics also know that students learn from not only what is taught in school but also from what is *not* being taught. They also ask: Should current controversial topics be discussed in schools? If so, how should the new curriculum be delivered? What is the message sent to students if "hot" topics are ignored in today's schools? And what is the message to students if the school budget is shrinking and new, important instructional material cannot be added to the curriculum because of the lack of funds?

By asking difficult and challenging questions, educational leaders can expose the hidden curriculum. Armed with this new knowledge, with the help of teachers, staff, parents, and the community, they have the possibility of developing curriculum that is truly in the best interests of their students. Educational leaders can make changes in their schools using a number of lenses and/or approaches. For example, they can turn to the ethic of care and develop, with the help of Noddings (1992), a school with a caring curriculum. Noddings has offered educators a framework for a general education curriculum organized around themes of care rather than the traditional disciplines (p. 173).

Educational leaders can also turn to the work of Starratt (1994a) and build an ethical school with a curriculum that takes into account the lenses of justice, critique, and care. This curriculum gives teachers and students ample time for discussions and projects that "will serve to nurture the basic qualities of autonomy, connectedness and transcendence in developmentally appropriate ways" (p. 68).

Additionally, educational leaders can consider the "real-world" ethics advocated by Nash (1996). This kind of ethics "is a complex admixture of personal, social and professional morality" (p. 1) and is grounded in applied ethics. The study of meaningful and current ethical dilemmas could be of importance not only to students but to teachers, staff, and the community as well.

This chapter contains four cases. In the dilemma "AIDS and Age-Appropriate Education," parents complain about a sixth-grade poster project that is part of a mandated class on AIDS education. State law requires some type of instruction. The posters are very creative and some have real condoms on them. There are pregnancy problems in the school, but some parents complain to Mr. Thompson, the assistant superintendent for curriculum, that they do not want their children exposed to these posters. Mr. Thompson is in a quandary as to what to do.

"Vivisection: A Classroom Physiologist's Dilemma" addresses advanced placement high school students' problems with pithing of frogs. Animal rights' issues are pitted against human rights' issues and the teacher is placed in a difficult situation. Here, teachers and administrators have to deal with their own beliefs as well as those of the students. The director of curriculum also has to reflect on the traditional curriculum that still provides appropriate training for future scientists and doctors regarding the pithing of frogs, compared with an alternative approach that could take into account students' and society's increasing awareness and support of animal rights.

"School Budget Blues and Copyright" focuses on a district with a shrinking school budget where teachers cannot order the materials they need to do their jobs well, and at the same time they are unable to duplicate material because of copyright laws. Recently, the principal sent out a memo reminding teachers about the copyright legislation. In this case, an outstanding teacher is caught by the principal duplicating materials. The principal is aware of the difficulties placed on the teacher who is desirous of providing her class with current instructional material, yet he is very concerned about violating the law.

"There's No Place Like School" illustrates problems that happen when regular classroom teachers are reluctant to be involved in inclusion programs that require that students with disabilities be educated in the same classrooms as all other children. The hard decisions administrators must make in assigning teachers as well as students are stressed.

AIDS AND AGE-APPROPRIATE EDUCATION

Eugene Thompson, assistant superintendent for curriculum at the Meadow Woods Consolidated School District, was not sure how Dr. Rose Jones, the superintendent, would side on this issue. He knew Dr. Jones was supportive of a K–12 sex education program, but Mr. Thompson also understood her desire to "keep the peace" with the public. Mr. Thompson's concern began when a few parents of sixth-grade students at the district's Forest Middle School objected to posters hanging outside the health room. The parents noticed the posters during the school's Back to School Night. They complained about the posters discussing how to have safe sex. The parents told him how some even had real condoms as part of the poster.

Mr. Thompson knew the posters were in that school's hallway, but he did not actually give it much thought, especially because the health education teacher, Marcus Fine, reminded him of the curriculum for the seventh-grade AIDS unit. It stated, "All students shall understand ways to prevent acquired immune deficiency syndrome (AIDS) without the instructor placing bias on either abstinence or the use of contraceptive devices." It was Dr. Jones who had pushed for this curriculum unit just 3 years earlier, and it had been unanimously approved by the district's curriculum committee and supported wholeheartedly by the school's principal, Susan Kaplan. Mr. Fine justified the poster project as a creative approach for students to understand the ways to prevent the transmission of the AIDS virus. He also noted that this project was for the seventh grade and not the sixth grade.

Before Mr. Fine left the Back to School Night event, Mr. Thompson approached him with the parents' concerns. Marcus Fine asked, "Why are the sixth-grade parents complaining to you? This is a project for the seventh-grade students."

"Look, Marcus, the parents feel their sixth-grade students are too young to be exposed to that type of message. They feel their children do not need to be exposed to such graphic representations of how to prevent AIDS. They also believe we are only promoting the use of condoms while not attempting to promote abstinence. They have already called the superintendent's office, and I'm sure we'll both be getting a call from Dr. Jones soon."

"With all due respect, Mr. Thompson," Marcus replied, "I had approached you regarding this project and you gave me the okay. Look, this poster's message is loud and clear, 'BE SMART, JUST SAY NO. ABSTINENCE IS THE SAFEST WAY TO PREVENT AIDS.' I've attempted to be supportive of students who wish to prevent the spread of AIDS—from both sides of this issue."

"Marcus, I understand that, but I am also concerned about Dr. Jones' response to the parents. The parents are going to focus on the posters that blatantly state, 'USE CONDOMS.' This is the type of poster the parents find offensive. They believe their kids are too young to be exposed to condom posters in the school hallways."

Mr. Thompson left the discussion feeling that Mr. Fine was unwilling to understand the other side of the issue. He realized Marcus Fine had conducted some controversial lessons in the past, but knew this one could become heated in the community. Even though the state mandated lessons on AIDS education, it was not too long ago that the school board banned some of the library books dealing with sexuality and the human body. The board justified that move by saying they acted on the opinions of the community.

The next day, Mr. Thompson began receiving phone calls from a few parents of current fourth-grade students. They were concerned about this poster project for next year because their children would be moving into Forest Middle School for fifth grade due to overcrowding at the grade school. Mr. Thompson listened to the parents' complaints. They felt that 10- and 11-year-old children should not be exposed to the explicit message of safe sex. They said it was in "poor taste" and an "obvious decay of moral values in our society." How could the district condone such immorality? Mr. Thompson listened to the parents and mentioned that he also believed it was a little young for fifth graders to be exposed to such sexual messages. He conveyed to the parents the district's policy on instruction of sex education to all the grades. He emphasized that discussions on the use of condoms was not in the curriculum for the fifth and sixth grades. Even so, the parents made it perfectly clear that their children should not be subjected to such safe sex posters for next year.

Mr. Thompson later heard from the superintendent. Dr. Jones wanted to meet with Mr. Thompson and Mr. Fine the following day to discuss the posters. She gave direct orders that Mr. Thompson take the posters down before she arrived at the school. Although she had heard only the parents' side of the issue, Mr. Thompson realized Dr. Jones was in no mood to debate, and he felt it was best to follow her orders. He knew Mr. Fine would not be pleased with this directive, but understood it could be considered insubordination if he did not adhere to Dr. Jones' request.

As he walked down to Mr. Fine's room at the end of the day, he passed two seventh-grade girls in the hallway. One was 8 months pregnant. He wondered what message was *really* being sent if the posters came down.

Questions for Discussion

1. Who decides at what age various parts of the curriculum should be introduced? At what age should students be exposed to explicit ways to prevent AIDS and pregnancy?

2. Is there a commonly accepted age when teachers can have students do an assignment such as the one presented? How do teachers or administrators know where to draw the line? Should the community have input into the specifics of the school curriculum? When, if ever, should the concerns of some community members become school policy?

3. If Dr. Jones had not even seen any of the posters, how could she know the posters were inappropriate for the middle school students? Does Dr. Jones have legitimate concerns over the next year's incoming fifth-grade class?

VIVISECTION: A CLASSROOM PHYSIOLOGIST'S DILEMMA

BioTech is a new charter high school funded through the state with support from a nearby university and several locally based, national pharmaceutical companies. BioTech's charter establishes it as a school aimed at preparing students for further training en route to careers in the health and science fields.

In an advanced placement biology class at BioTech High School, several of the laboratory activities require freshly pithed frogs that students use to perform experiments on the functioning frog heart. Frogs are anesthetized prior to pithing to prevent pain and suffering. Biology students take this activity very seriously; experimental success requires careful dissection to expose the frog heart without damaging surrounding organs and vessels. The first stage of the pithing process renders the frog brain dead, and the second stage reduces skeletal muscle reflex activity.

Specifics of the pithing procedure are not described here because many laboratory manuals include a procedure similar to a classic "source-book" for biology teachers by Morholt, Brandwein, and Alexander (1966). Several additional experiments that require fresh tissue do not necessitate pithing, but do require careful dissection to remove tissue from a freshly killed frog (e.g., a sciatic nerve). For these procedures, most students prefer to use a decapitated frog instead of a pithed (brain-dead) frog.

In general, biology teachers and students are finding it increasingly difficult to justify vivisection. Consequently, students at BioTech are not required to perform or observe the pithing process, but they are encouraged to work through the experimental vivisection procedures with their laboratory group. Biology students have extensive dissection experience with preserved specimens, but their experiences and responses to vivisection are varied. Some students are not willing to observe vivisection, whereas others are willing to observe but not perform vivisection. Only a few students are willing to perform the procedure. These students often indicate that they find the experience to be less traumatic if the frog has been treated with an amphibian anesthetic prior to pithing and vivisection. Students are not in agreement on the vivisection issue, and experimental groupings are usually sufficiently diverse to provide constructive debate among group members. The following dialogue highlights the issues surrounding "live dissection." Ahn contemplates a career in medical technology. She refuses to observe the procedure. Rodney plans to major in premed and eventually become a physician. Rodney is willing to perform the procedure and is attempting to convince Ahn that live dissection is necessary.

Ahn: I refuse to hurt that frog!

Rodney: The anesthetic has knocked him out—won't feel a thing. Besides, pithing renders the frog brain dead.

Ahn: That is not the issue! What gives us the right to take this frog's life, and for what purpose?

Rodney: For months I have been dissecting stinky rubbery preserved specimens. I plan to attend medical school, and I'm going to try my hand at this procedure. If I can't handle it, I better find out now!

Ahn: I'm sure you can handle it . . . you big *brute*! What makes our species superior to other species?

Rodney: *Think* about it, Ahn. I am sure the frog can't! . . . Or can he? Do you think that doctors never practice?

Ahn: It is not necessary for this frog to be sacrificed so that *you* can become a doctor, or to find out if *you* have the stomach for medicine. Besides, no medical procedures should be performed unless the result is expected to extend life.

Rodney: Oh! Well, in that case, I'll sew him back up!

Ahn: *You are hopeless!!* I'll be back after the procedure.

Rodney: Why should I share my data with you if you don't contribute to the activity?

Ahn: Because the teacher said that I may instead use a new computer program that simulates the effects of acetylcholine and adrenaline on the frog heart.

Rodney: Fine for your purposes, but I plan to use this herbal extract as an additional independent variable—find *that* in your computer simulation!

Ahn: What practical application might your herbal extract have? It is unlikely that *you* would stumble on some amazing substance by accident!

Rodney: If I did, would this frog's death be justified?

Ahn: Depends how amazing the substance is . . . but just experimenting with no practical application in mind is *not* justified.

Rodney: But that is what basic science is all about.

Ahn: Well, Mr. Serendipitous . . . you do your thing and I'll do mine.

Questions for Discussion

1. Do animals have rights? Do we, as human beings, have a responsibility to species other than ourselves?
2. What are the pros and cons of pithing frogs? If you were Director of Curriculum at BioTech High, would you permit this procedure? Would your answer be different if the animal were one other than a frog, such as a dog? a cat? a horse? Why or why not? How would you decide where to draw the line?
3. Pithing frogs is legal, and sometimes considered to be a good practice. Do these things make it also ethical? Why or why not?
4. If pithing frogs was the only way to improve medical practice and save human lives, would that justify the practice? What if it were not the only way, but was clearly the best way, would your answer change? Why or why not?

SCHOOL BUDGET BLUES AND COPYRIGHT

The Pierpoint School District had undergone major changes in the past 5 years. The student population had more than doubled with no signs of stopping. A new superintendent had come on board and construction had begun on three more buildings. The additional students, materials, buildings, and staff needed each year to accommodate the overwhelming growth was staggering. Each year the budget process grew more tense and territorial as departments fought for the few available dollars. Dr. Sharif, principal of Valley View High School, knew this year's budget would again be tough and bare-bones. What the board and superintendent were demanding seemed impossible.

In compliance to the central administration's request, the following year's school budget was originally submitted without any allowances for inflation, additional students, or the expenses that accompany them. Now central administration was mandating further cuts from every school. The faculty had been complaining about the concessions they were already forced to make. Dr. Sharif knew he would bear the brunt of teacher anger and criticism for this new round of cuts. As far as the cuts for his school were concerned, the only fair thing to do would be to take an equal amount from each department.

Throughout the past few years, cost-cutting measures had been put in place in all of the district's operations, presumably to ease the need for additional funds. One major and highly controversial cost-cutting measure was the introduction of a central copying center to be used by the entire district. Although there would still be a copier housed in each building, the large, multiple classroom copying needs were to be sent to the central copying center. Teachers were reminded that even though there had been cuts in instructional materials, they were not to make copies of copyrighted material.

Dr. Sharif continued to agonize over which items to cut from each department's budget request, when he began to hear noises in the outer office. It had been hours since the office staff had gone home, and the custodians had already cleaned the offices. Dr. Sharif immediately went to investigate and found Jane Tharp, one of the school's most dedicated and well-respected teachers, in the outer office. An instructor of instrumental music, Ms. Tharp had stopped in after a band rehearsal to use the office copier. She was startled by Dr. Sharif's sudden appearance. As Dr. Sharif drew closer, Ms. Tharp appeared to be trying to hide what she was doing. When he was close enough, Dr. Sharif could see that Ms. Tharp was copying music for one of her bands. Dr. Sharif was dumbfounded. Not only was this against district policy, but it was illegal. The superintendent had recently sent a memo to all district employees reminding them about the legalities and liabilities of making photocopies of copyrighted materials.

Ms. Tharp immediately began to try to rationalize her deed by pointing to the rising cost of music, the number of students in her bands, and the declining budget money.

Questions for Discussion

1. Is anything truly wrong with what Ms. Tharp is doing? Is she being dishonest? Is she stealing? Explain your answer.

2. Do you think Dr. Sharif is concerned because the superintendent might uncover what is happening? Because the publishing company might possibly find out and he would be held personally liable? What other reasons might there be for

Dr. Sharif to be concerned? Would your answer as to what Dr. Sharif should do change depending on his motivations? How would it change?

3. What do you see as the reasoning behind copyright laws? Who do they protect? What are the consequences of violating them? Are they just laws?

4. What action do you think Dr. Sharif should take? What is your reasoning? What would be the most fair decision Dr. Sharif could make? Fairest for whom? What would be the most caring decision? What parties should Dr. Sharif consider in making a caring decision? Explain your logic.

5. Do you think Ms. Tharp's actions would be easier, or harder, to justify if she made multiple copies of music for personal use, to give to her friends? If she were not a good teacher? Why?

THERE'S NO PLACE LIKE SCHOOL

It was that time of year again. Mrs. Stell sighed as she considered her task. As supervisor of special education, she needed to guide the assignment of students receiving special education services to regular education class lists for the upcoming year. Her task was made considerably more difficult at Kessler Elementary due to the number of children with special academic, emotional, and behavioral difficulties moving from third grade to fourth. Further complicating her task were the number of teachers less than eager to take on these added responsibilities without the benefit of direct help from learning-support teachers. She had but one special education teacher per grade available. She considered the recent history of the district, specifically the last 5 years. She knew that although momentum was building to move past the difficulties, the district still had many changes to make.

Simonsville and Kessler Township are considered part of Hailysburg, one of the fastest growing areas of the state. Until recently, a large steel mill in nearby Blairsville employed many of the area's residents. With the mill's decline, employment lies mainly with smaller factories, companies, and small businesses in the area. The Kessler School District enrollment numbers approximately 2,100 students housed in four buildings. Two buildings are located in the Borough of Simonsville and two in Kessler Township.

Hampton, located in Simonsville, has approximately 430 kindergarten through second-grade students. Students move from Hampton to Kessler Elementary. This building, with approximately 470 students in the third to fifth grades, is located in Kessler Township. Students attend Grade 6 through Grade 8 at Kessler Middle School located in Simonsville. Kessler High School's student body numbers 670 and is located in Kessler Township. The School District General Characteristics Profile lists the population of the school district as 96.99% White.

Most of the buildings are old and in need of renovation. The district has chosen, as an alternative, to undertake a huge building project that will combine the entire enrollment in a single complex on one campus. This building project, which began in October 1997, aims to maximize the use of the buildings for all the students and the community.

During the past 13 years, the district has had seven different superintendents during eight periods of leadership. One period in particular sparked great contention. The superintendent had been, while assistant superintendent in another district, instrumental in implementing inclusive practices. At Kessler, he decreed that all children, to the maximum extent possible, would be taught in the regular education classroom. In the past, the district had an unusually high proportion of identified students with individual education plans (IEPs) suggesting a pointed belief in the "placement" of students with special needs. Previously, personnel of the intermediate unit (IU) provided special education services in pull-out programs. Beginning in the 1993–1994 school year, the district assumed responsibility for its learning support students, and immediately many of these began to be included in regular classrooms.

This sudden move to inclusive practices caused substantial dissension in the district. This was a radical departure in philosophy for a district whose special education population exceeded that of the national average. Indeed, during the past 4 years, the Middle School and Kessler Elementary had had special education populations double that of the national average. As a result of the superintendent's mandate, most students labeled as students in need of learning support were placed in regular education classrooms. Learning support teachers ran from classroom to classroom trying to deliver one-on-one instruction to all of the students.

Additionally, some members of the school board locked this superintendent out of his office in response to an alleged directive by him that principals attend a meeting where a speaker with a political agenda would be presiding. This action resulted in a court case, much publicity, and growing distrust among the board members, community, teachers, and administration. The upheaval had far-reaching aftereffects. The current and assistant superintendents, respectively, both in the district less than 18 months, are still picking up the pieces. Indeed, they were hired for the express purpose of getting Kessler School District back on track. They have begun the slow process of developing mission statements and goals and reforming instructional and curricular practices with the entire staff. As a result of this lack of continuity of leadership, each school within the district has been handling special education services in differing ways. There is little congruency of practices among the schools.

Mrs. Stell has been a faculty member for 30 years. Due possibly to the existing bad feelings concerning inclusion, she has done little to advocate for the philosophy. Rather than mandating the practice, she has allowed it to develop naturally. Truth be told, she had had doubts about its appropriateness. However, she has seen inclusive practices and coteaching allow more students, including those with IEPs, to reach greater achievement.

After its initial impact, progress toward implementation of an inclusive philosophy at Kessler Elementary had been slow. For the past several years, all children with learning or emotional support disabilities were placed with the two most agreeable and cooperative teachers at each grade level. Thus, the same two teachers at each grade level have a disproportionate number of labeled students each year. A special education teacher provides these two grade-level teachers support. Children in need of more extensive services have been placed outside the district.

This move toward inclusive practices has been only partially successful. Certainly, the teachers involved feel that students with special education labels belong in the regular education classroom, but there is still little co-teaching and much "pull-out." Generally, students are pulled out of the regular classroom and instructed in small groups in a separate room for a large portion of the major subjects, such as reading and math. At first, teachers were less inclined to make modifications and adaptations in the classroom, yet, as a few teachers became more comfortable with the practices, their use became a bit more frequent. This practice, unfortunately, did not spread through the entire faculty. However, many teachers, when planning for the following year, work to ensure that "their kids" are placed with those teachers who do make accommodations and modifications and have the support of a special education teacher. As a result, two teachers at each grade level have a preponderance of children who are at risk of failure.

Mrs. Stell recalled conversations she had had with Mrs. Mitchell, a fourth-grade teacher. "I love working with a co-teacher. With two of us in the room, we're able to generate more ideas, observe more about each student, and provide more remediation *and* enrichment." Mrs. Stell sighed again. Mrs. Mitchell and her co-teacher Mrs. Freed clicked. They both felt that the "specially designed instruction" mandated on their students' IEPs could occur in the classroom. Not so the third- and fifth-grade teachers. Mrs. Chase expressed those teachers' sentiments well when she said, "Sure these students get a lot by just being in the regular education classroom, but they can't do the work the regular education students are doing. They need their own materials and instruction at their own levels. And they're so easily distracted, we have to go to another room." Mrs. Stell wondered when these teachers would think about a systematic process of achieving IEP goals within the context of typical classroom instruction and understand that not all students had to be doing the same thing at the same time.

This year, the situation became intolerable for two third-grade teachers. One, Mrs. Brandle, had five children with IEPs in addition to several other children who were at risk. The other, Mrs. Carou, had 7 children, out of 25, with IEPs. Both teachers found that not only did these children have academic needs, but they had behavioral and emotional difficulties as well.

Mrs. Carou started her teaching career as an emotional support teacher. She is devoted to her students and enthusiastically strives to ensure their success. She can very ably articulate what each student is capable of achieving. Additionally, she is quite capable of providing differentiated instruction in her classroom ensuring that all children will succeed. Despite the difficulties of meeting the needs of her students, it is obvious that each child has made progress.

For Mrs. Carou, this year has been exhausting, to say the least. She began early in the year to make faculty aware that although all of her students were making progress, keeping the students with IEPs in just two classrooms next year would do them and the other students a disservice. She was clear and emphatic about these beliefs.

At Kessler Elementary, Mrs. Stell, the guidance counselor, the instructional support (IS) teacher, and the principal met with the learning support teachers, the regular education teachers who worked with the students with IEPs. The discussion revolved around how best to serve the needs of all students next year. It was evident from the start that the fourth-grade teachers did not agree with Mrs. Carou's recommendation. Most felt that centralizing the children with IEPs was more desirable because it allowed the special education teacher to more effectively deliver direct instruction. It would enable her to work with the students, plan, and co-teach with both the regular education teachers.

When Ms. Marco, the new IS teacher, questioned why spreading the students out among all of the classrooms was not considered, Mrs. Chemsky exclaimed, "We did that before and it didn't work. Because the students were all at different levels, it was a nightmare for the learning support teacher to try and get to all of them and teach them reading and math. She simply couldn't get around to all the students." Ms. Marco seemed puzzled. "When you look at the instructional techniques, activities, materials, or assessment, modifications can be made in a methodical manner allowing most of our students to have their educational needs met within the context of regular classroom instruction." Most of the teachers greeted her statement with a blank stare. She tried again. "When you plan for instruction with your co-teacher, don't you look at using the least intrusive modifications first?" Many in the group started talking at once. "There was no time to co-teach". . . . "Planning . . . when could we plan?" . . . "The kids couldn't read, in the first place, how could they do any of the worksheets?" . . . "The kids need one-on-one instruction." Ms. Marco related her experiences as a third-grade teacher and learning to make adaptations for all of her students.

At this point, Mrs. Stell tried to engender a conversation about the idea that students receiving special education services did not necessarily need one-on-one instruction from the learning support teacher. Rather, whenever appropriate, instruction should be immersed in the instruction for the entire class. Co-teaching allowed, even encouraged, this to occur. Mrs. Stell could see that most of the teachers emphatically agreed with Mrs. Chemsky. However, it was certainly clear that all felt that there was not enough support. More teachers and aides were needed to meet the needs of the students with IEPs.

Although the group clearly articulated the need for additional staff, the reality was that there was not enough money to hire more teachers or aides. It was not that the administration and board did not see hiring as important, but with the desperately needed building project, there just were not enough resources. This ad hoc special education task force continued to meet to discuss how best to place the students. When discussion focused on placement in two classes versus more classes, Mrs. Stell's comment to the faculty was that placement should be based on students' needs.

Mrs. Stell, the guidance counselor, Mrs. Carou, Mrs. Brandle, the learning support teacher, and the instructional support teacher studied options to optimize placement of students at-risk and with IEPs for next year. After much discussion and debate, it was clear that to best increase achievement for all, the students should be spread among the six fourth-grade classes. The classrooms had been separated into two groups. Three classes would contain the children with IEPs that had more intensive need and would receive direct service from the special education teacher. The other three would contain the children whose IEP goals could be met by the regular education teacher in consultation with the special education teacher.

There remained a problem: Mrs. Clay. She had been teaching fourth grade for 27 years. She felt that students should be held to a high standard of expectation and that those students who could not meet the standards should be placed elsewhere. She felt inclusion perpetrated a grave disservice on both regular education students and students with IEPs, placing undue pressure on the latter and also slowing instruction for the other students. She vehemently disagreed with the inclusive philosophy, vociferating that those children did not belong in her classroom.

Mrs. Stell considered her options. She could place the students in all fourth-grade classrooms and tell Mrs. Clay that she is responsible for teaching all children. Remembering an article she had recently read and agreed with, indicating that one bad year can affect a student's academic career long afterward, could she possibly consign a child to that possibility? If she did place children with IEPs with Mrs. Clay, she had two options. She could give her the children who would need more intensive adaptations and the part-time help of the learning support teacher. Alternatively, she could give her a class where the needs were not as intensive, but in which case she would receive very little direct support. Otherwise she could choose not to give her any children who were at-risk or had IEPs. This last option would probably ensure that students who were at risk would have good fourth-grade experiences. It would also make the other teachers' jobs more difficult. Additionally, it did nothing to move the school toward the philosophy by which all children can learn and all children belong.

Questions for Discussion

1. What are the benefits and drawbacks of placing students in need of learning support in Mrs. Clay's classroom? What are the benefits or drawbacks to placing them in other classrooms but hers? Does Mrs. Stell need to consider Mrs. Clay's professional beliefs before placing students in her classroom? Why or why not?

2. If Mrs. Stell refrains from placing students receiving learning support in Mrs. Clay's classroom, how might that affect the school community? How do the students' and parents' wishes play into this problem?

3. If Mrs. Clay is assigned students with learning support, what support should the principal and Mrs. Stell offer? If Mrs. Clay is not assigned students with learning support, what role will she play to affect change toward a more inclusive philosophy?

4. What does the law say about placing students receiving special education services in regular classrooms?

5

Personal Codes Versus Professional Codes

Deborah Weaver
William W. Watts
Patricia A. Maloney

In this chapter, we explore the thorny problem of what happens when an individual's personal code of ethics differs from her or his professional code and/or the standards of the profession. This chapter raises personnel issues that go well beyond the people involved in the dilemmas. In these dilemmas, educational leaders are forced into positions in which they may have to draw the line between an individual's personal and professional life.

In chapter 1 of this book, the ethic of the profession was introduced as a paradigm and described in some detail. This ethic was discussed as a fourth paradigm for viewing and solving ethical dilemmas. Whereas the ethics of justice, critique, and/or care have been emphasized as paradigms by different scholars in educational leadership, rarely is the ethic of the profession treated as a separate and discrete model. In this book, however, a case has been made for professional ethics to be defined as a paradigm that includes ethical principles, codes of ethics, professional judgment, and professional decisionmaking.

Shapiro and Stefkovich (1998), in an earlier work, stressed the importance of asking educational leadership faculty and students to formulate and examine their professional codes in light of their personal codes and the codes of professional standards and national, state, and local organizations. They are not alone in this emphasis. Duke and Grogan (1997), Mertz (1997), and O'Keefe (1997), to name but a few, also encouraged a similar process.

The professional paradigm is based on the integration of personal and professional codes. However, frequently an individual's personal and professional codes collide. This makes it difficult for an educational leader to make appropriate decisions. Shapiro and Stefkovich (1998), in their research of doctoral students in an education administration program, found that there were many conflicts both between and among students based on their professional and personal ethics. Not only were the conflicts among students, but they were within oneself. In analyzing codes, Shapiro and Stefkovich and their students thought it was important for educational leaders to look for consistencies and inconsistencies between and within their own personal and professional codes. Clashes were also discovered when an individual had been prepared in two or more professions. In this case, codes of one profession might be different from another; thus, what serves an individual well in one career may not in another.

The three cases presented in this chapter offer the reader an opportunity to think through the decision-making process involving dilemmas that arise when an individual's personal ethics conflict with the professional ethics associated with public education. The cases highlight the paradoxes between personal codes and professional codes. Additionally, the questions posed at the end of the cases encourage the discussion of other paradigms in relationship to personal and professional codes. The ethics of justice, critique, and care can be applied to the dilemmas in this chapter. Educational leaders sometimes cross paradigms in their personal and professional codes but are not aware of this until they spend the time to develop and reflect on their beliefs.

In the ethical dilemma "Drunkenness or Disease?" a director of special education has been convicted of drunk driving. He is an alcoholic and the community wants him fired. Legally, the school district can do this because the state law says that school personnel may be fired for criminal convictions. However, the assistant superintendent for personnel is ambivalent because the individual is very effective in his work and has been for a long time. Additionally, the assistant superintendent believes this individual is suffering from a disease requiring support and assistance.

"Rising Star or Wife Beater?" focuses on a health and physical education teacher and coach of high school football, wrestling, and baseball who is well regarded by the school superintendent and is in line for a new and important position. The administrator finds that the teacher has been brought up on charges of domestic abuse. Although he has had the greatest respect for the teacher professionally, the superintendent now is beginning to feel differently about the teacher on a personal level. Many angry parents have heard about the teacher's domestic behavior and ask for his dismissal at a school board meeting. The superintendent is faced with a difficult decision that he is asked to make in a public forum.

In the third case, "Job-Sharing: Some Real Benefits," we are introduced to an administrator who must balance the needs of employees and the guidelines of her board of education. This case involves a pilot job-sharing program in a district in which the teachers' union now demands full-time benefits for a year of part-time work. The union makes the case that currently only married people can afford to job-share without a proper benefits package. This case resonates with the assistant superintendent for personnel on a personal level because she is single and would like to support benefits for unmarried people. However, professionally, she is aware that the job-sharing arrangement could establish a precedent enabling all part-time workers to request benefits. For the assistant superintendent, any decision made in this case may have repercussions that will affect her at the personal level and especially at the professional level in her relatively young career.

DRUNKENNESS OR DISEASE?

Dr. Mari Wang sat in her office long after the school day had ended, contemplating the most recent problem that had occurred in the Harrison City School District. Since becoming an assistant superintendent for personnel 5 years earlier, she had had her share of problems, but never one involving a key administrator, especially one whom she had supported for the position.

Mr. Kidder presently held the central office position of director of special education and had done so for the past 4 years. He had been a superstar special education teacher and had earned a master's degree and a supervisory certificate some years ago that qualified him for the position when it became vacated through a retirement. Mr. Kidder not only interviewed well, but was the teachers' first choice, having earned their respect and support during his 20-year service to the district as a classroom teacher as well as chairperson of several special assignments. In addition to his ability, Mr. Kidder possessed a charming and gregarious personality that often made it easy for him to develop an instant rapport with staff as well as parents. Dr. Wang had to admit he often brightened her day with his stories, jokes, and optimistic attitude about life in general.

How sad that this was not the case today. In fact, just 2 hours previously, Mr. Kidder looked like the world had come to an end, and Dr. Wang was the only link saving him from a fate worse than death. Mr. Kidder's career was in jeopardy; he was about to go to jail because he had been arrested a few weeks earlier for drunk driving. To make matters worse, it was his third conviction, punishable by a 3-month imprisonment in the local county jail.

The court decided that due to his position in the school district, his character witnesses during the trial, and the lack of any other illegal convictions, he would be eligible for the work-release program, pending approval from his place of employment. Mr. Kidder explained that he would arrange to have someone pick him up at the prison in the morning and bring him to work. He would be able to work until 5:30 p.m. each day, when someone would take him back to the prison by the required curfew of 6 p.m. This would be the arrangement for the next 3 months, which would take him to the end of May.

After the specifics of the court's recommendations and subsequent plans of Mr. Kidder, Dr. Wang felt it necessary to question Mr. Kidder about his actions and why he would allow himself to be put in such a situation in the first place. Obviously embarrassed and ashamed, Mr. Kidder revealed that he had finally admitted to himself that he was an alcoholic. He was not sure when it had all started but the pressures of the job and an unstable marriage had been a lot to handle on a daily basis, so he had gotten into the habit of stopping at a local tavern for a drink or two after work. After the first two arrests, he sloughed it off as just being unlucky that he was caught and paid the fine. He had had a couple of drinks but certainly was able to drive safely. He really felt that he was not doing anything wrong and that the law was unfair, too strict, and the result of political pressure groups.

The third arrest, coupled with the seriousness of the consequences, made him take a hard look at what he was doing to himself. He went on to say that he had taken the first step to recovery by attending an AA meeting and had recently stood up and admitted that he had an alcohol problem. It was his intention to sign himself into an alcohol recovery program, through the district's employee assistance benefit program, after the school year ended. This would involve 6-weeks during the summer, which also happened to be his vacation allotment.

Mr. Kidder was confident that he would be able to return to work, well on his way to recovery, and that this type of incident would never reoccur. He was extremely apologetic for his actions and any embarrassment it might cause the school administration and was hopeful that the district would support his plans for recovery from this disease. Dr. Wang thanked Mr. Kidder for his candidness and told him she would get back to him with the decision of what action she would recommend to the superintendent and Board of School Directors the next day.

Dr. Wang realized this problem had many facets to review before coming to a decision. She knew she was in for a long night.

Questions for Discussion

1. Do you see Mr. Kidder's problem mainly as a disease or a lack of moral fiber? Explain your answer. Do you believe that as a teacher Mr. Kidder should be held to a higher moral standard than ordinary citizens? Why or why not? Should what Mr. Kidder does in his private life make a difference in his job status? Why or why not? Does it make a difference that he is a good teacher? a good administrator? a good colleague? Where would you draw the line between what is of public concern and what is strictly private when considering school employees?

2. Suppose that the law was politically motivated; does that make a difference as to what Dr. Wang should do? Do you believe the law is unjust? Too strict? Why or why not? Who does the law benefit? If the law were unjust, should that make a difference as to Dr. Wang's decision?

3. What would a caring person do in Dr. Wang's place? To whom should care be directed; are there others who should be considered in addition to Mr. Kidder? Who?

4. Do you see this dilemma in the same way as the next dilemma about a coach who beats his wife?

RISING STAR OR WIFE BEATER?

Alex teaches health and physical education in Maple Grove, an affluent school district. He is also a very successful high school football, wrestling, and baseball coach for the district and is recognized by many coaches throughout the state as an exceptional coach. Many of Alex's teams have won conference and state titles during his tenure. His athletes admire and respect him and revere him as a father figure and role model. A large percentage of his athletes earn athletic scholarships to attend major colleges and universities. Some have gone on to careers as professional athletes. Many people—parents and students alike—feel a great deal of gratitude toward Alex for all of his time and effort in coaching, particularly Superintendent Brown.

Alex began his career as a substitute teacher in Maple Grove, making himself available to the school district at all times. He substituted in all subject areas as well as in physical education classes. He worked with all grades, and even volunteered his services to chaperone school activities such as dances, class trips, and any athletic event he was not coaching. He gave up his evenings and weekends to do what he could for the district in hopes of earning a permanent teaching position that provided him with a contract and stability in his chosen profession. He was motivated and determined to earn a teaching position as soon as possible. After 3 years of substitute teaching, Alex began experiencing frustration and depression because he had not attained a full-time teaching position. However, a position was soon to open and a contract would be awarded as well. In the interim, Alex continued to substitute as well as to coach football, wrestling, and baseball. Alex was particularly fond of coaching football and was considered an expert. Not only was Alex a talented coach, he was very committed to coaching a winning program.

At the end of the school term, the teaching position Alex desired would be advertised, and applicants would start interviewing for the position. All of Alex's hard work and effort would soon pay off. A permanent teaching position and head coaching job were imminent. Even the assistant principal of the high school phoned him and offered his endorsement for the position. The interview process proceeded as scheduled. Alex's interview was nearly flawless. The very next day, Alex received a phone call from the high school principal, Mr. Young, and was offered the position. Alex was ecstatic.

Alex thought Monica, his wife, would be pleased as well. The couple have two children. They live in a lovely home in the district and both children attend the district's schools. Their older child attends the high school and is actively involved in many activities and their younger child attends one of the elementary schools. Monica has a teaching degree in special education and also works for the district as a substitute teacher. There have been days when both Alex and Monica taught together in the same building and had their older daughter in class. On these days, both Alex and Monica acted very professionally and went about their responsibilities as usual.

By all appearances, Alex and Monica seemed like the ideal couple and consummate professionals. Alex continued to excel at coaching, and the students in his classes all liked him very much. Superintendent Brown and Principal Young were very pleased with his recent evaluation and considered making plans to train and groom him for a future administrative position.

Monica seemed content to substitute regularly and was willing to start coaching a sport if the opportunity presented itself. Administrators were beginning to take notice of her positive teaching style and her ability to work well with students. However, although Alex and Monica's professional lives appeared stable and happy, their private life, especially their marital relationship, was undergoing serious difficulties.

In the ensuing weeks, Alex and Monica had many fights and arguments at home. Their marital problems continued to escalate, and the stress began to have an effect on Alex's professional obligations and responsibilities. Alex was exhibiting a short temper with his students, colleagues, and even some parents. His physical appearance was disheveled and rumors that alcohol could be smelled on his breath were being passed about. Colleagues noticed that he often arrived late to school and late to some of his classes. His athletes also saw a change in his behavior at practices and were very concerned.

Principal Young also noticed these changes and immediately requested a conference with Alex. In their meeting, Alex confided to Principal Young that he and his wife had separated. He said it was a temporary situation and he felt a reconciliation was soon to occur. Alex apologized for his lack of professionalism the past few weeks and assured Principal Young that it would not happen again. Superintendent Brown was informed of the matter but was not overly concerned.

The following week, Superintendent Brown received a phone call from the school district solicitor, who informed him that Alex was arrested the previous night for assault and battery of his wife. She was not seriously injured during this incident and, therefore, decided not to press charges against her husband. Because the school year was coming to an end, Principal Young and Superintendent Brown decided not to make an issue of the incident. They also felt that the summer break would ease any community concerns about what had happened. Besides, Alex's reputation in the district was very positive, and he was the football coach. He did not need any bad publicity.

During the summer break, Alex had another altercation with his wife and was again arrested for assault and battery. This time, his wife decided to file and press criminal charges against Alex. She even contacted her attorney to begin divorce proceedings. Her decision to press charges resulted in headlines in the local newspaper, thus alerting the community, school board members, and school officials to the situation.

The news of Alex's arrest spread quickly throughout the school district. Many parents were angry and very concerned about the situation. A group of parents organized to discuss their concerns and agreed to go to the school board to demand the resignation or firing of Alex. Reports indicated that more than 100 parents signed a petition supporting Alex's dismissal and that they planned to storm the next school board meeting in protest.

Shortly after Alex's arrest, his wife once again decided to drop the charges. District officials took the news at face value. They did not think about the cycle of battering as it affected this case. They even put aside their concerns about the community discord over the matter. School officials felt that at the upcoming board meeting, a few parents would voice their opinions over this incident, then the meeting would proceed as scheduled. School officials, however, underestimated the outrage community members were experiencing.

More than 100 parents attended the board meeting. There was standing room only, and the line of people outside the door continued to get longer. A feeling of tension permeated the room as parents discussed their anger about the situation. School officials and board members were getting nervous and were quite concerned with what would take place in the meeting.

As the meeting got under way, one parent blurted out, "Get rid of Coach Alex; we don't want this type of person teaching our children." The other parents in the room started to cheer and yell their concerns. The president of the school board quickly hammered his gavel on the desk in an effort to bring the meeting back to order.

As the voices of angry parents lowered and the meeting came to order, the president of the Parent–Teachers Association, Mrs. Lewis, stood up and spoke on behalf of the concerned parents. In a calm, soft, articulate manner, she praised the accomplishments of Coach Alex. She was careful to address all the positive things he contributed to the success of the school, students, and the athletic program. She even mentioned how he had helped her son earn an athletic scholarship to college. But she stated firmly, "Regardless of his past record, we cannot tolerate such acts of violence from any of our teachers." She continued by saying that teachers are role models to students, and parents entrust their children to people believed to be of high moral character. She concluded by saying, "It is very clear that Coach Alex has violated our trust, and therefore, we ask for his dismissal." With that, she turned toward Superintendent Brown and asked, "What are you going to do about this?" The people in the auditorium instantly became silent. Superintendent Brown knew that these people were very upset and wanted a response. It was obvious that Superintendent Brown had an extremely difficult decision to make.

Questions for Discussion

1. What is the fairest choice Superintendent Brown could make? The most caring?

2. One might decide to give Alex the job based on a "greater good for the greater number" reasoning in that he has helped so many young athletes. What are the strengths and weaknesses of this argument? Do you agree with it? Why or

why not? What course of action would be in the best interest of all students? Of the student athletes at Maple Grove High? As a coach, does Alex have a special responsibility to be a role model for his students? Is this responsibility more than that of a teacher who does not coach?

3. Compare Superintendent Brown's dilemma with that of Dr. Wang in the previous scenario. Could it be argued that spousal abuse is a disease as alcoholism is a disease? Why or why not?

4. Alex has yet to strike a student. Is denying him the job a good preventive strategy? Why or why not? Do you see any ethical problems to this reasoning. If not, why not? If so, what are they? Should a person's private life be just that, private? Why or why not?

5. What questions might a critical theorist ask in this situation? On what concerns might she or he focus?

6. What would you do if you were Superintendent Brown? Explain the reasoning behind your answer.

JOB-SHARING: SOME REAL BENEFITS

Dr. Marisa Garcia is a single, 35-year-old, assistant superintendent for personnel in the Birchwood School District. She has been in her current position for less than a year. Prior to her appointment as assistant superintendent, she was an assistant principal and a classroom teacher in the same district. Dr. Garcia is happy in her current position and usually enjoys the daily challenge of her work. However, today was an exception. As she drove home from a school board meeting, she had to admit that it was difficult to find enjoyment in solving her current dilemma.

The teachers' union had requested a meeting with the school board to negotiate several changes to the school district's employee job-sharing benefit. Before the meeting with the union, Dr. Garcia met with the school board. Mr. Bob Johnson, head of the board's personnel committee, made it quite clear that the school board was not interested in any changes at this time. He then noted that Dr. Garcia was expected to make a recommendation to the board following her meeting with the union to enable the district to prepare for negotiations.

Mr. Johnson owned a small business that had not been very profitable, but it had been successful enough to put food on the table. He was always complaining about the cost of insurance and other benefits he had to provide for his own employees. He often voiced his opinion about teachers being "spoiled," especially when he compared education to the business world. He had been known to say, "This is a small town and the taxpayers are getting real angry about how much the teachers get compared to other workers."

Because contract negotiation was one of Dr. Garcia's responsibilities, she was the administrator who would be meeting with the teachers' union. Although she had never been involved in a contract negotiation from the administrative side of the table, she knew the teachers had no bargaining power. The job-sharing benefit was presented by the union last year. The board adopted it as a 1-year pilot program; therefore, it was not officially negotiated into the contract, and the current contract was still in effect for another year.

The meeting began with a review of the current guidelines for job-sharing. Although James Jacobs, the union president, was extremely intelligent and an excellent teacher, he often argued for the sake of a good argument, especially with Marisa Garcia. Mr. Jacobs had a problem with Dr. Garcia's quick ascendancy through the hierarchy. It had been rumored that Mr. Jacobs informed a few union members that this would be an easy sell, insinuating that Dr. Garcia would not be able to hold her ground against him.

After reading the guidelines, Mr. Jacobs requested the first modification. Two other union representatives in attendance remained silent for most of the meeting except to discuss among themselves or echo Mr. Jacobs' sentiments. Dr. Garcia agreed to the first modification, as it was merely a change in the wording of a sentence. The second request was not so easy.

Under the current guidelines, a full-time teacher interested in job-sharing gives up full-time status for 1 year. The current teachers' contract states that part-time employees do not receive medical benefits. Therefore, any teacher involved in a job-sharing situation is not eligible for benefits. The union was requesting a revision of this provision. The union felt strongly that the provision was not fair and it did not provide equal opportunity to all teachers. The union felt the district was discriminating against teachers based on marital status because only teachers with spouses who were employed and received medical coverage would be able to take advantage of the benefit.

Dr. Garcia did not respond to the claim of violating equal opportunity; however, she informed the union representatives that the board would not support the revision of the job-sharing benefit that maintained medical benefits. Part-time employees did not receive benefits in this district. If the district did provide benefits for the job-share employees, then all of the part-time employees would expect benefits. The district could not afford to extend benefits to part-time employees. The union countered by saying that the difference is that the job-sharers are full-time, tenured employees and deserve to maintain their benefits: "We don't believe the union can accept it any other way; we represent the entire faculty— not just those who are married with two incomes."

Dr. Garcia then asked, "Are you saying you are rejecting the current proposal?" Although she cared deeply about this issue on a personal level, she knew what her professional strategy should be for this meeting. Thus, she began by explaining that there were three teachers requesting the job-sharing for next year.

Receiving this new piece of information, Mr. Jacobs replied by saying, "Rejecting it would not be fair to those teachers. We will accept it. However, the language should read that the district agrees to extend the pilot for a second year." Despite their personal differences, in Dr. Garcia's opinion, James Jacobs raised a few valid arguments. Dr. Garcia knew that, on one hand, she had really wanted to advocate for single people being able to take advantage of this opportunity; on the other hand, she wanted to uphold the guidelines as directed by the school board. Upholding these guidelines would also show Mr. Jacobs who was in charge.

Dr. Garcia knew how important this decision was to her young career as assistant superintendent. What if her recommendation forced a teachers' strike? Or what if her recommendation made the board think she was just another woman who was indecisive and willing to extend job-sharing indefinitely under the guise of a pilot program? In order for Marisa Garcia to clearly understand her own position and make a recommendation to the board, she knew that she had to determine if equal opportunity as well as care and concern were afforded to all teachers in the district.

Questions for Discussion

1. What are the possible courses of action Dr. Garcia might take? Of these, which is the most "just"? Why? Which is the most caring? Why? In this situation, must there be a conflict between what is just and what is caring? Explain.

2. Dr. Garcia is a single woman with her own personal convictions regarding this matter. What would you expect these convictions to be? Should they enter into Dr. Garcia's judgment of the situation? Why or why not?

3. If benefits are extended to job-sharing individuals, should they then also be extended to other part-time employees? Why or why not? Who do you suppose initiated the job-sharing program? Who benefits from it? Who is left out?

4. From a caring perspective, how should Dr. Garcia address Mr. Jacobs' concerns? Mr. Johnson's concerns? How would you answer this question from a justice perspective? Must these answers be different? Why or why not? If you were Dr. Garcia, what would you do to resolve this dilemma?

6

The American Melting Pot Versus the Chinese Hot Pot

Patricia A. L. Ehrensal
Robert L. Crawford
Joseph A. Castellucci
Gregory Allen

In this chapter, administrators face challenges that extend well beyond the school and move into the home. These dilemmas ask educational leaders to not only think through their own responsibilities and behaviors but also take into account students' and parents' behaviors and especially their backgrounds.

In this chapter, the paradox between the American melting pot and the Chinese hot pot is highlighted. Many of us are familiar with the metaphor of the melting pot. It emerged as an aftermath of the popular play by Zangwill (1910). The play, *The Melting-Pot*, presented an acculturation model molding immigrants into a "predetermined standard of desirability" (Wong, 1993). Along with this concept, the national motto of *e pluribus unum*—from many, one—also conveyed this desire to create Americans from a "dizzying array of peoples, cultures, and races" (Sewell, DuCette, & Shapiro, 1998). The metaphor of the melting pot left it to the schools to educate students from many cultures through a common language, a common history, and common goals, principles, and values. The schools bore the burden of producing the social and cultural integration required to create "real Americans."

But what is meant by real Americans? What is the ideal American who should emerge from the melting pot? Judging by the writings of Cushner, McClelland, and Safford (1992), this concept seems not to have changed for more than 100 years. They wrote:

Real Americans are white and they are adults: they are middle-class (or trying very hard to be); they go to church (often Protestant, but sometimes Catholic as well, although that is a bit suspicious); they are married (or aim to be) and they live in single-family houses (which they own, or are trying to); they work hard and stand on "their own two feet"; they wash themselves a good deal, and generally try to "smell good"; they are patriotic and honor the flag; they are heterosexual; they are often charitable, only expecting a certain amount of gratitude and a serious effort to "shape up" from those who are the objects of their charity; they eat well; they see that their children behave themselves. (p. 216)

Despite the emphasis on acculturation through the schools and other institutions, there have also existed other forces in America such as the distinct languages, histories, goals, principles, and values of different ethnic groups that emerged from the community, the home, and the individuals themselves. For many minority groups, then, in this age of diversity, the melting pot metaphor no longer seems viable. Instead, the concept of the Chinese hot pot (Tek Lum, 1987, p. 105) may be a better fit for their view of American culture. In the hot pot, although all the foods are cooked together, each maintains its unique flavor and texture. The transition from the metaphor of the melting pot to the hot pot has not been easy or smooth. Tensions and inconsistencies exist that can lead to paradoxes or dilemmas. For example, schools, on one hand, want students to understand and appreciate other cultures, while on the other hand, they want to socialize young people to make them into American citizens.

The cases presented in this chapter illustrate paradoxes between the dominant culture of the melting pot and the different cultures of the hot pot. They challenge the reader to examine the conflicts that occur when the dominant culture in U.S. schools comes in contact with subcultures and "other" cultures. Two questions worth considering are: Which party has the greater share of social power? What are the assumptions the school leaders have about "other" and their cultures in each case?

After reading each of the dilemmas that follow, it is important to take the time to consider the questions at the end of each case. Hopefully, these questions challenge the reader to reflect on the dilemmas from the perspectives of the ethics of justice, critique, care, and the profession.

The first selection, "A Home for Marlon: The Foster Child Case," serves to demonstrate how difficult it can be to determine where the language of rights is rejected and a dialect of care is embraced. Here, a school's director of pupil personnel services must choose between laws and responsibilities and relationships as he determines whether to tell his friend, a teacher, harmful information about a foster child's background for whom the teacher is providing a home.

In "Parents' Rights versus School Imperatives," a principal witnesses a father spanking his son at school. The father is working class and well meaning and the son has many behavioral problems. The parents are divorced and the father has custody of the son to save him from a bad situation with his mother. The principal is legally bound to report this incident as child abuse to the proper authorities and yet he questions making the report.

"Responsibility and the Organization" involves George, a Jamaican student who attends a music magnet school and is quite talented. However, he is receiving mediocre grades because he has many family commitments related to music. (This is how the family supports itself.) The student's father is angry because George has received Cs in music primarily due to absences. The father wants the teacher to change his son's grades because he feels it is unfair to penalize him because he is performing. Yet, would this be fair to the other students?

A HOME FOR MARLON: THE FOSTER CHILD CASE

Marlon, a 16-year-old-male classified as emotionally disturbed, enrolled at the Benjamin Franklin High School in September and was assigned to a self-contained special education classroom. Marlon had been relocated into the district to be placed in a new foster care home. He had been in various residential placements and foster care homes since the age of 10. Marlon was removed from his biological parents after it was discovered that he was the victim of their sexual and physical abuse. Marlon's student file contained reports documenting 3 years of increasingly disturbing behaviors. He was demonstrating an escalating pattern of frequent fire-setting behaviors, and had reportedly sexually molested two young children with whom he shared a foster care placement.

Jim Campbell, the school's director of pupil personnel services, is concerned because Marlon's new foster parents are Mr. and Mrs. Kearns, a well-respected, kind couple who fit in well with this conservative, church-going community. Mrs. Kearns is a part-time art aide at the high school. Mr. Kearns is a businessman who frequently travels and works long hours. They have two young children: a 6-year-old girl and a 3-year-old boy. Mr. Campbell has frequently socialized at the Kearns' home for birthday parties, dinners, and other family activities. He has young children like the Kearns family. As per foster care state law and policy, Mr. and Mrs. Kearns have not been informed of Marlon's past history and behaviors.

Resolved to make things right, Mr. Campbell quickly left school the day he first read Marlon's student file firmly convinced that he knew the right thing—the only thing—to do. Although sure in his conviction, Jim also knew he should not act immediately. He needed time to evaluate the situation, in order to make a reasoned decision. Walking through the school parking lot that afternoon, he was clear on one thing. No way was he going to permit the Kearns family's two children, children just like his own, to be potential victims of a sexually aggressive, emotionally disturbed youth. Although he felt a need to wait until the next day to make a decision, he felt certain that his desire to protect the Kearns family would primarily inform his decision.

Later that evening, with his children tucked away and his wife asleep early with the flu, Mr. Campbell decided to give the issue deeper consideration. As he settled under the covers, he thought about his own children safely tucked in their beds. He also hoped for the safety of the Kearns children. Before turning out the bedside lamp, Jim read over the Personal and Professional Code of Ethics he had written down some time ago, now kept as a book mark in his Bible. What caught his attention was a particular line. It read: "Always be a voice, a presence for the comfort and protection of the weak, the innocent, the defenseless . . . because there but for the grace of God go I. . . ." And there but for the grace of God so went his children. However, unlike the Kearns family, they did not have this threat of a stranger in their home as they slept.

Mr. Campbell knew he had to tell Mrs. Kearns about Marlon's past, about the potential danger now posed to her children. Mr. Campbell was a deeply religious, family man who valued his children, and all children, immensely. He began his career as a teacher because of his desire to help children. The care and protection of students was central to his moral code.

As he lay thinking of the Kearns' children, Mr. Campbell was confronted with the image of Mrs. Kearns crying in his office, telling him the details of how Marlon one night had done the unspeakable to one of her children. He then saw himself confessing that he was sorry, that he knew about Marlon all along. Perhaps, if he had revealed to her the truth, her tragedy could have been avoided. Jim saw a tearful Mrs. Kearns challenge him, "You knew, you knew about this all along and you did not tell me! How could you let this happen to my children?"

Then something else began to creep into his thoughts. Even as he imagined Mrs. Kearns condemning him, he remembered that, in addition to being a concerned father, he was also a man with a very serious professional responsibility. In his current role as director of pupil personnel services, he began to feel a certain uneasiness. In one sense this was not an unfamiliar position for Mr. Campbell. He certainly had been aware of other situations in the past that were similar or worse, involving issues such as sexual abuse, incest, drugs, and domestic violence. Although he had been disturbed, he had never before been tempted to violate students' privacy and confidentiality, even though some of the situations had been actually much worse than the Kearns family's current situation.

His thoughts about confidentiality led him to consider consequences. "And what about the consequences of my actions?" thought Mr. Campbell. "I've never violated a student's confidentiality before. Credibility demands honesty. If word got out that I told the Kearnses about Marlon, how would my teachers and the other students feel? Would they feel confident that they could talk with me confidentially? Would I still be credible in their eyes?"

"Beyond credibility," his thoughts continued, "are there any legal ramifications if I violate the laws governing student privacy? Would this jeopardize my current position? Would I be passed over if I ever wanted to become superintendent?" "Foolish!" he screamed inside, "We're talking about children here. Maybe all these confidentiality laws protecting juvenile criminals weren't good laws in the first place!"

Mr. Campbell was becoming more concerned and physically upset at this seemingly unsolvable dilemma. He did not even want to look at the clock, knowing all too well that it was much too late to claim a good night's sleep. He again recalled his Personal and Professional Code of Ethics. "Always be a voice." But for whom was he supposed to be a voice? Who was supposed to receive the charity, mercy, forbearance, and benevolence that he mentioned in his code? What did these words really mean anyway? Mr. Campbell began to wonder about Marlon. Was he asleep or was it a sleepless night for him also?

Mr. Campbell wondered how many sleepless nights—nights of turmoil and fear—Marlon had suffered in his young 16 years. Wasn't Marlon a victim, too? Perhaps it was Marlon who really was the weakest, most defenseless voice in this whole mess. The Kearns' children, like Mr. Campbell's own children, had warm, stable, loving homes, but what was it like to be moved from home to home as a child? The reality of the situation, beyond all the worries, was that only one child had been repeatedly victimized. And that child was Marlon.

Mr. Campbell, under his warm covers, felt thankful for the security and comforts of his own home. "If I told Mrs. Kearns, she would immediately have Marlon removed from her house." So where would Marlon go next? Another move, another school, another strange room during another sleepless night? A sinking feeling hit Jim. A deeper sadness, not anger, just sadness for Marlon. Marlon did not seem such a monster now. In fact, he did not really know Marlon at all, just what Marlon's records said and what his own fears had portrayed Marlon to be.

Mr. Campbell imagined Marlon reporting to his office prior to leaving the school due to another move, another transfer into another foster home. He saw himself seated at his desk in his office. Before him stood Marlon, who with tired eyes simply said, "You told them about my past. They weren't supposed to know. I wanted to start all over again. I just wanted what every other kid has, a home. I've already been hurt too many times by adults I trusted. How could you do this to me?" As he continued to reflect, Jim did not know what bothered him the most, his own anger or his own tears.

Despite the difficulty, Mr. Campbell knew he must view the current dilemma from a more objective perspective. Thus, a fundamental question remained: Did Marlon's presence in the Kearns' home pose a grave danger to the Kearns family? First and foremost, he considered that although Marlon may have a past history of dangerous behaviors, including fire setting and sexual molestation, he had not yet demonstrated harmful behavior or expressed intent to engage in harmful conduct. Marlon had not yet crossed the line to suggest he posed a grave risk to the Kearns family.

The dilemma for Mr. Campbell was based partly on emotional identification and affinity for the Kearns family and the projection of his own fears concerning Marlon. The situation that objectively confronted him at this juncture involved only the potential of dangerous behavior and his own fears. Marlon had not shown any indications to warrant concern for the Kearns family.

Mr. Campbell clearly agonized over this decision. Neither course of action relieved him of responsibility for potential adverse consequences. All night he tossed and turned. And as he did, he constantly asked: What would be the best way to resolve this dilemma? How could he reach a decision that would be in harmony professionally and personally?

When the morning dawned, Mr. Campbell finally made his decision. He decided not to tell Mrs. Kearns about Marlon's past. His reward was simply a sense of relief stemming from the feeling that his decision was in harmony with who he knew himself to be, as both an administrator and a person.

Questions for Discussion

1. Do you think Mr. Campbell made the best decision? Why or why not? If you were in his place, what would you have done?

2. Assume that Mr. Campbell did not personally know the Kearns family. Would that factor make a difference in your opinion as to the best course of action? Why or why not? What if Mr. Campbell did not know the Kearns family but knew Marlon very well. Should that factor make a difference in his decision?

3. Consider this case from the point of view espoused by Kohlberg (1981), Gilligan (1982), and Noddings (1984). How might the decision have played out considering each of these theorists?

4. Mr. Campbell chose not to break his state's law regarding confidentiality of foster children's records. Do you agree with his decision? Is it ever justifiable to break a law when making an administrative decision? When? Do you see any way that breaking the law might have been justifiable in this case?

5. Was Mr. Campbell's decision in Marlon's best interests? In the best interests of the other students? In the best interests of the community? What community? Do you see any conflict between what appears to be Mr. Campbell's personal and professional codes of ethics? Between his codes of ethics and his actions? Explain.

PARENTS' RIGHTS VERSUS SCHOOL IMPERATIVES

It was 4 p.m. on Friday afternoon and Ned Parker was still at his desk. Before him was the pamphlet distributed by the Division of Youth and Family Services that detailed the school's role in preventing child abuse. Among other things, the pamphlet was very specific with regard to school officials' responsibilities. Any school official or teacher who fails to report suspected child abuse, the pamphlet read, could be held criminally liable.

Of course Ned Parker was well aware of the legal responsibilities of school officials with regard to suspected child abuse cases. Indeed, he had presented in-service training to his teaching staff on just that subject. As principal at Sandalwood Elementary School, Ned had reported dozens of suspected child abuse cases over his 8-year tenure. He understood his responsibilities all too well. Yet on this particular Thursday afternoon, he felt very unsure of himself. Earlier that day he had witnessed a parent beating his child, but was hesitant to report this incident as child abuse.

The child in this case was Robert Buck, a sixth grader who was both small in stature and emotionally immature for his age. He had transferred to Sandalwood earlier in the school year from a district in another state following the bitter divorce of his parents. Robert's father, Frank Buck, had been awarded full custody, and the transition was anything but smooth.

Robert was a discipline problem almost from the first day he arrived. He was constantly disrupting his classes, disrespectful to his teachers, and both physically and verbally abusive to his classmates. Needless to say, his academic achievements were few. Robert had been a frequent visitor to Ned Parker's office and had been rapidly progressing through the various levels of the school discipline policy.

Frank had also been a frequent visitor to the school. He was a rough and relatively uneducated working-class man who had dropped out of high school to marry his pregnant girlfriend. When the marriage went sour, he made every effort to gain full custody of his only child to remove him from what he called the "unhealthy influence of his mother." In his dealings with Frank, Ned had believed him to be a concerned parent who was doing his best with the child under very difficult circumstances. He had personally come to the school each time there was a problem with his son. His meetings with the principal and each of Robert's teachers had always been cordial, and he had often expressed support for the school's efforts toward his son. He regularly attended parent back-to-school nights and was one of the few fathers active in the PTA.

It was becoming apparent that Robert was not responding to the typical disciplinary practices of the school. After a series of disruptive behavior reports from teachers, Mr. Parker suggested to Frank that he implement a behavior remediating program suggested by the school psychologist. All indications were that Frank was dutifully following this program.

The final straw came early on Thursday when Robert was sent to the principal's office for what his teacher described as behavior that was out of control. Ned called Frank to inform him of the problem. Angry, Frank said "This has gone too far. That boy needs to be taught once and for all how to behave." With that, he abruptly hung up the phone.

Ned did not quite know what to make of that phone conversation until Frank appeared at his office door no more than 20 minutes later. With a facial expression clearly displaying anger and frustration, he apologized to Ned for the trouble his son had caused. "Now I'm going to do what I promised if I had to come out to this school again," he said to the boy. With that he grabbed his son's arm and jerked him out of the office and down the corridor. Ned followed him out and was horrified at what followed.

When they got to the end of the corridor, Frank threw his son up against the wall and began thrusting a pointed finger in his chest. Ned could barely make out

CHAPTER 6

what was being said, but it sounded angry and threatening. Then Frank forcefully turned his son around and began spanking the boy across the backside no fewer than eight times. Pain and embarrassment were evident on Robert's face as tears streaked down his cheeks. Ned yelled down the hall, "Please, sir, that is not necessary." Frank bellowed back, "I'll decide what is necessary for my son." With that he grabbed Robert by his shirt collar and marched him out the door.

Now, Ned Parker sat in his office contemplating whether he should report the incident as child abuse. On one hand, he thought, he had clearly witnessed behavior he himself would never condone in himself or any of his teachers. The brutal nature of the spanking was also disconcerting and clearly painful to the boy. And who knows what kind of beating Robert might receive in the privacy of his father's home.

On the other hand, it was only a spanking. As a boy, Ned himself had been spanked countless times for misbehavior by his father. Yet he would never consider his father a child abuser. Many parents spank their children routinely and would be appalled at any suggestion that they were committing child abuse. Anyway, what business does the school have interfering with parents' rights to discipline their own children as they see fit?

Ned knew what the consequences would be if he reported this incident to the Division of Youth and Family Services. The division routinely filed child abuse charges against parents for cases with less evidence than this one. The children were typically placed in a foster home until the case was resolved in court. Parents were usually fined and forced to undergo counseling and parenting classes. In the most extreme cases, the child could be removed from the home permanently.

Ned also knew the consequences of not reporting a suspected child abuse case. He remembered an incident from a few years before in a neighboring school district where a man mercilessly beat his 10-year-old daughter to death for accidentally breaking a dish. School officials were accused of neglecting to report suspicions of abuse that they held for months before the child's death. Ned did not want to be held responsible for another such atrocity.

Nevertheless, Ned believed Robert's father was a concerned and loving parent who had given in to personal frustration over the continued misbehavior of his son. After all the other disciplinary alternatives had failed, he probably resorted to carrying out a standing threat. Was it really child abuse or merely a good and well deserved spanking? Is it right to make this father answer for his actions in a court of law and possibly face losing his son? Is it ethical to ignore this incident and possibly enable this father to severely hurt his son? Ned stared at the phone on his desk and wondered whether he should make that call.

Questions for Discussion

1. Do schools have the right to determine how parents may discipline their children? Do you believe Mr. Buck's actions consititute child abuse? Why or why not? How do your state laws define child abuse? Should Mr. Parker report this in-

cident to the authorities? Why or why not? If Ned thought Mr. Buck's actions were not child abuse, but feared that Mr. Buck was, or could become, more violent at home, should he report the incident to the authorities? Discuss the pros and cons of taking action against an anticipated wrong-doing.

2. What do you suppose was the purpose of states instituting child abuse laws? Who likely supported or rallied for such laws? Who do these laws benefit? Do you believe such laws are fair? Why or why not? If there was a class difference between those who fought for the law and those whom the law affected, would that change your opinion of the laws? Why or why not? Should exceptions be made in these types of cases or should the law be followed literally? Explain your answer. Should professional judgment be a consideration in reporting such incidents? Why or why not? How would this work? Whose professional judgment should be taken into account and why those persons as opposed to others?

3. What is the most caring solution to this problem? Would it be caring to report Mr. Buck? What solution would be in Robert's best interests? The best interests of all students?

4. Some 27 states have passed laws forbidding corporal punishment in schools and many, if not most, school districts have policies against this type of discipline. Discuss the pros and cons of corporal punishment in schools. Is there a difference between corporal punishment in schools and similar types of discipline at home? Explain. Is there a difference between corporal punishment and child abuse? How are they the same? Different?

RESPONSIBILITY AND THE ORGANIZATION

George Woodley and his musical family had recently arrived in the United States from the island of Jamaica. His father, John, was in the process of finding a high school for him to attend. Because of George's keen interest in music and piano skills, it was important to Mr. Woodley that his son be placed in a high school with a worthwhile music program. George auditioned for the Westfield High School Music Magnet Program and was accepted. He was asked to give performances in both piano and voice.

George's vocal selection was acceptable, but could be described as throaty with a nasal quality. This was partially due to the reggae style of singing that his family had performed for many years. Nevertheless, it was decided that George would be placed in the vocal component of the music magnet program at Westfield High. At the time of his son's audition, John Woodley had made it clear that his son would have to miss performances because of the family's professional obligations. This was a major concern because the grades of vocal students are based on their participation in class as well as performances.

As the year progressed, George's effort in class was minimal. He was beginning to miss performances consecutively and would announce that he would not be participating in a performance the very day of the engagement—which Mr. Henderson, the choir director, saw as unfair, especially to the other students. As a result of George's minimal participation in class and lack of attendance at concerts, Mr. Henderson calculated his grade to be C.

John Woodley became furious on discovering that his son received such a mediocre grade. Consequently, he made an unannounced visit to the school to voice his displeasure. He stated, "My son could have gone to virtually any school, and this school really is beneath him."

Mr. Henderson told Mr. Woodley that George was at Westfield High by choice, and the music program was certainly not inferior by any means. Mr. Woodley felt very strongly that his son should have received a grade of A simply because of his advanced music skills and performance experiences. Mr. Henderson made it clear to John Woodley that the criteria that he deemed appropriate for assessing George's music grade would not suffice.

In his second year at Westfield High, George's performance and participation in choir did not improve significantly from the first year. Mr. Henderson felt he had been more than fair in determining George's grade. Could he continue to allow George to neglect his academic responsibility because of family musical commitments that John Woodley claimed were a major source of income for the immigrant family? Just how was Mr. Henderson to handle this situation without being unfair to the students who seemed to expend much more effort than George?

Several students overheard Mr. Henderson and George in discussion immediately following choir class one day, at which time the latter attempted to plead his case for a grade of A. The students became incensed by what they heard, and began to speak their opinions on the matter. Mr. Henderson controlled the situation by discontinuing the conversation and sending the perplexed students to their classes.

Questions for Discussion

1. To what extent should George be responsible to his family? To his school? Where do his greater responsibilities lie? How might George's dilemma be interpreted through Kohlberg's (1981) theory? Through Gilligan's (1982)? Through those of other theorists?

2. Who made the rule that all students should be judged on class participation? Where would the basis for such criteria lie? Is this a fair rule? Fair to whom? Who does the rule benefit?

3. George knew the rules regarding grading up front; was he then not obligated to abide by them? Why or why not? Would your answer be different if George had not been told the rules ahead of time? George's father had informed Mr. Henderson of George's family obligations from the beginning. Should this knowledge require or expect Mr. Henderson to treat George differently from other

students? Should some students be treated differently from others? Why or why not? Discuss the pros and cons of such individualized treatment. From an ethical perspective, how does one know where to draw the line?

4. What are George's rights? His parents' rights? Should a school change the rules because one parent objects?

5. What do you personally believe should happen in this situation? What do you as a professional in a school believe should happen? Are these answers the same or different? Why?

6. What solution to this dilemma would be in George's best interests? In the best interests of the other students? Do these answers have to be different, or is there a solution that would satisfy both? All parties concerned?

7

Equality Versus Equity

James K. Krause
David J. Traini
Beatrice H. Mickey

In this chapter, the cases presented deal with issues of inclusion, seniority, and access to educational opportunity. In all these dilemmas, the administrators in charge want to do the right thing. But what is right for one person or group might not be good for others.

In the diverse and complex society of today, a paradox exists between the concepts of equality and equity. We define equality under the rubric of equal or even-handed treatment as discussed by Strike, Haller, and Soltis (1988). They provided this definition: "In any given circumstances, people who are the same in those respects relevant to how they are treated in those circumstances should receive the same treatment" (p. 45). Equality, defined in this way, looks at the individual and the circumstances surrounding him or her. It does not focus on group differences based on categories such as race, sex, social class, and ethnicity. This view is one of assimilation because it assumes that individuals, once socialized into society, have the right "to do anything they want, to choose their own lives and not be hampered by traditional expectations and stereotypes" (Young, 1990, p. 157). It is a positive and inspiring concept—an ideal that is well worth attaining.

Equity, on the other hand, as we define it here, deals with difference and takes into consideration the fact that this society has many groups in it who have not always been given equal treatment and/or have not had a level field on which to play. These groups have been frequently made to feel inferior to those in the mainstream and some have even been oppressed. To achieve equity, according to Young (1990), "Social policy should sometimes accord special treatment to groups" (p. 158). Thus, the concept of equity provides a case for unequal treatment for those who have been disadvantaged over time. It can provide compensatory kinds of treatment, offering it in the form of special programs and benefits for those who have been discriminated against and are in need of opportunity.

Movements have had a profound effect in fighting for equity or social justice. In the case of the Native American movement, a battle took place against the concept of assimilation. This fight was for "a right to self-government on Indian lands" (Young, 1990, p. 160). It also was a desire to retain the language, customs, and crafts that gave this group its special identity.

Pressure from group movements has often led to legislation that has provided opportunity. To give an example of this, the women's movement fought for and eventually obtained the passage of Title IX of the Education Amendments of 1972. Title IX made it known that discrimination on the basis of sex was illegal in any educational program receiving federal funding (American Association of University Women, 1992, p. 8). The passage of Title IX opened the door for many gender equity programs and projects (American Association of University Women, 1995) enabling women and girls to be empowered and learn how to overcome the barriers that still exist today.

But it is not only in the area of racial, ethnic, and gender movements that the paradox of equality versus equity can be found. If one turns to the umbrella term of diversity and defines it broadly, then a range of differences can be explored that includes categories not only of race, ethnicity, and gender but also of social class, disability, sexual orientation, and exceptionalities (Banks & Banks, 1993; Cushner, McClelland, & Safford, 1992; Shapiro, Sewell, & DuCette, 1995).

The paradox of equality versus equity is treated differently under each of the four paradigms that we use to analyze ethical dilemmas in this book. Turning to the first of the four paradigms, the ethic of justice is broad enough to include both equality and equity. This all-encompassing definition goes back as far as Aristotle. He "held that justice consists in treating equals equally and unequals unequally" (Strike & Soltis, 1992, p. 46). By this, Strike and Soltis felt he meant that "if high-school grades are the basis of admission into a university, then two people with the same grades should receive the same treatment. Either both should be admitted or both should be rejected" (p. 46). This illustration demonstrates the use of the justice paradigm for the principle of equality.

But Aristotle also recognized that "when people differ on some relevant characteristic they should be treated differently." Strike and Soltis (1992), in this case, provided the example of a visually handicapped student who is not being treated fairly by being given the same book to read as a sighted student. "Here" they said, "fairness requires different treatment" (p. 46). This illustration utilizes the concept of equity in relation to the paradigm of justice. Thus, under the ethic of justice, both equality and equity are acknowledged.

The ethic of care, another of the four paradigms used in this book, challenges the impartiality and detachment of moral reasoning (e.g., Gilligan, 1982; Noddings, 1984). The concept of impartiality has tended to work by distancing oneself from others to enable an equal weighing of all interests. The caring frame would not be remote, but instead would be empathetic and place equity rather than equality at its center. Those who care no doubt would really listen to the voices of diverse groups—particularly those who have been discriminated against in the past. They would turn away from the ideal of impartiality that is inherent in our society and our beliefs (Young, 1990). Instead, they would recognize differences and the history of unfair treatment to different groups over time by trying to rectify past wrongs.

Under the ethic of critique, hard questions can be raised concerning the treatment of diverse groups in society. These questions can take into account the issues of oppression, domination, and discrimination. The myth of merit (Fishkin, 1983) and the problems of distribution of goods and services to all groups within our society can also be explored. Additionally, within this paradigm, current demographic trends can be considered in critical as well as positive lights. The unprecedented expansion of our nation's racial, ethnic, socio-economic, and cultural groups can be discussed and questioned using this ethic, as can some of the accompanying problems of children of poverty, single-parent homes, and students of exceptionality (Hodgkinson, 1992; Utley & Obiakor, 1995).

Turning to the ethic of the profession, we know that how our schools address the evolving needs of our students and society will determine, to a great extent, the success of our nation in this new millennium. A great challenge to be faced involves how educators balance the acceptance and support of difference without hurting the collective whole of our society. This is not an easy balance for educational leaders to attain. And the major question in this paradigm remains: Is equality or equity, or a combination of both, in the best interests of the students?

In this chapter, dilemmas are presented in an attempt to evoke analyses of ethics related to equality and equity issues. A range of approaches are addressed in the cases themselves and in the questions that follow each dilemma.

The first case, "When All Means All," deals with a problem in a school that is beginning to serve as a model of inclusion for the state. In this dilemma, the problem centers around an emotionally disturbed child in a regular elementary school classroom who has caused chaos. Having worked with the child in the classroom for a time, a teacher has found him to be a constant source of problems. She feels that the child is infringing on the rights of others and is also not receiving the kind of attention that he needs in an inclusive classroom.

In "Black and White and Shades of Gray," new minority teachers are to be retrenched because of economic reasons. The old rule of equity, "last hired, first fired," is presented with all of its problems. The principal is placed in a very difficult position in a district in which minority students are increasing in number.

In "Access to Knowledge," a principal is approached by Latino parents who want their child to take courses in the college preparatory track. The student has been discouraged by the guidance counselor and by his teachers from taking college preparatory work. The principal finds out that the student has not been doing well in his classes. Conflicting feelings on the part of the principal in handling the situation are discussed.

WHEN ALL MEANS ALL

As Jim Martin headed toward home, thoughts filtered back to better times. He found this occurring more frequently during the past few weeks. Three years had passed since the Freedom Elementary School had implemented a full inclusionary model of educating students with disabilities. As director of special education for the school district, and with his office in the Freedom building, Jim had invested a great deal of time in developing the program and, thus, had a special interest in seeing it succeed. He also believed that the process of inclusion was a natural extension of the child-centered, collaborative approach the district and community supported. Here, the regular classroom would be the educational setting of choice for all students. However, after its early success, more recent struggles were now wearing on everyone. "How could something that unified everyone such a short time ago be so divisive now?" he thought.

Jim had served as director of special education for 11 years. He was well liked and well respected by his staff and co-workers and had an excellent relationship with Rose O'Brien, the building principal. Jim had always prided himself on fostering the development of a highly skilled, caring faculty. He was able to do this by sharing leadership.

The idea of establishing an inclusive school stemmed from his work and that of a committed core of teachers. This team truly served as the driving force behind the exploration, development, and implementation of an inclusion model. It was not easy to build this concept into a functional process, but everyone's hard work and steadfast belief provided the foundation for what would benefit all. Support soon grew from a small pocket of Freedom's staff to widespread support throughout the faculty and community. The vast majority of teachers genuinely believed all children would be best served in a regular education setting with their same-age peers.

Eventually, Freedom's effort to include students with disabilities began to draw attention from across the state. Educators from other school districts began to explore the "Freedom Model." Administrators and teachers flocked to the school in droves. Faculty were asked to present at statewide conferences on inclusive practices. Jim had just recently received notice of the upcoming publication of an article he had written for a professional journal. It was entitled, "Freedom: An Inclusionary Model for All." Advocates of full inclusion held the Freedom Model as an example of successful practice that developed from the grassroots effort of caring educators.

Momentum from the early successes, or the "Golden Age" as it later became known, carried staff through the first 2 years. Inclusion was not an easy process, but challenges were met with effective collaborative efforts. Staff and services were in place to prevent any child from needing to be pulled out of the regular classroom. Students were doing well, and the parents of students with disabilities were happier than ever. Although there were some parents who voiced concern about unfair levels of attention directed toward students with disabilities (and away from their own children), these parents remained the minority in the Parent–Teachers' Organization. The school had established its identity as an inclusive school. This was a source of pride to the school and community.

At the start of the third year, Cody Smith, a fourth-grade student with serious emotional difficulties, enrolled at Freedom. Staff had included students with behavior problems in the past, but the level of Cody's conduct disorder was new to most. He had a long history of aggressive acting-out, disruptive behavior, and poor peer–teacher interactions. He had been previously served in a self-contained classroom for students with emotional disabilities. He had met with moderate success in this program, but the program's staff felt the need for continued extensive support.

The team met with Mr. and Mrs. Smith to review the wealth of educational and psychiatric information provided in Cody's file. Though there was some hesitancy, the team agreed that inclusion for all means all. If they were to be true to their established philosophy, they could not segregate certain students. The Smiths were somewhat confused by all this. Early in Cody's school career, they tried to fight Cody's removal from the regular classroom. Just as they were becoming comfortable with the separate services, a new set of professionals were saying the regular classroom would be best for their son. They liked the idea of him being with "normal" kids, but would he fit in? They were finally convinced to try an inclusive class after speaking with other parents who advocated strongly for inclusive education.

The team assembled the following week to develop a plan outlining the supports and services necessary to educate Cody in the regular fourth-grade classroom. A range of supports involving additional staffing, curricular and instructional adaptations, and behavior support planning were developed. Jim swelled with pride as the staff met this challenge and developed a quality, individualized program. Cody's parents were fully involved and very pleased with their new-found empowerment. During the first month in his new school, Cody experienced only minor difficulties. Adjustments in supports were made to address his needs, and he responded well. Everyone was excited to be part of another success story. Cody was happy, learning, and making new friends.

As October arrived, so did the firestorm of Cody's behavior. Almost overnight, he went from cooperative and pleasant, to aggressive and disruptive. He threw books and food, cursed openly at adults, refused to comply with basic requests, and threatened to hurt other students. Mrs. Appleby, his teacher, often found herself at his side or in the hallway trying to calm Cody and prevent further disruption. Everyone now knew what a conduct disorder involved. The team immediately pulled together for the first of seemingly endless team meetings.

The team adjusted Cody's behavior support plan to allow for "calming" time when he became agitated. This proved unsuccessful. Individual aide support was assigned. He continued to disrupt class with verbal outbursts. Teachers began to rotate one-on-one coverage. Unstructured time was studied and structured. The team studied factors in Cody's life that may have precipitated these difficulties. Profanity-laced tirades and noncompliance continued. Positive contingencies proved ineffective, family case management was fruitless, and medical intervention was unsuccessful. Consultation with social workers and psychologists led to little, if any, positive change.

After 3 months, the roof was about to blow off! Parents throughout the school demanded Cody be removed. Others requested that their children transfer to other classes away from Cody. An undercurrent opposing inclusion started to surface for the first time. Jim Martin danced from fire to fire, trying to quell the rising displeasure of staff, students, and parents. Throughout this, Cody and his parents remained pleased with the regular class placement.

Then it happened. The team wearily pulled together for another planning meeting. Jim was presenting his thoughts on the latest plan for intervention when Mrs. Appleby, Cody's teacher, stopped him midsentence and said, "I want him out of my class now! This is no longer fair to Cody or the other children." Two other team members concurred, "We cannot meet his needs in the regular classroom. He is too disruptive to the education of other students. This kind of class is too much for him to handle. He is too much for us to handle." Jim was completely caught off-guard by their comments.

"What about our philosophy that all our students will be included in the regular classroom?" Jim asked.

"Now!" they said with an angry glare.

Several other team members, including Cody's mother, wanted to hear more from Jim about possible interventions. Heated argument began to rise from the team. Accusations, name calling, and blame placing surfaced. Jim thought everyone could use a chance to cool off, so the meeting was rescheduled for the following morning. Members of the team stormed out spewing threats involving the local teachers' association and disability advocates.

Word spread quickly within the school and community. Jim's office was transformed into a mission control center. Staff marched in to vent their frustrations. Even Principal O'Brien, who had been a steadfast supporter, expressed serious concerns. Parents called to address a number of rumors they had heard. Advocates called for reassurance that inclusion would not be sacrificed. Cody's father even called to let Jim know his attorney would be attending the morning conference. What else could go wrong? The phone rang again and Jim recognized the superintendent's voice, and tone, on the other end. He didn't focus on every word, but the message came through quite clearly—fix this one immediately.

As Jim continued his drive toward home, he began to question his own beliefs regarding inclusion. "If we say inclusion is for all children," he thought, "is it

.it for us to separate some who are not experiencing success in this setting? Has .il this work gone for naught? Is the process worthwhile if anger and resentment become pervasive throughout the school? How can this situation be 'fixed' as the superintendent instructed?" He wondered what would happen at the next morning's meeting and every day thereafter.

Questions for Discussion

1. Considering the support Jim has lost, should he continue the program? Discuss the pros and cons of program continuation that Jim should consider before he makes his decision.

2. Is it fair to sacrifice the needs of the individual even when he or she represents a voice not represented by the majority? Is it ever fair to sacrifice the greater good for the individual? If so, under what circumstances? Is this the situation that exists with Cody? Does caring extend to the needs of the group or is it restricted to the needs of the individual? Where and how does one draw the line between individual rights and the common good? In this case, is there an ethical choice that would support both sides? If so, what is it?

3. There are important laws to protect individuals with disabilities, but there are also laws that require teachers to educate all children. Do you see laws as conflicting? Why or why not? Who made these laws? Who were they designed to protect?

4. Do you see any conflicts between Dr. Martin's personal beliefs about inclusion and his professional beliefs? What in this scenario leads you to draw your conclusion?

BLACK AND WHITE AND SHADES OF GRAY

Northern Regional High School District had changed dramatically in the past 10 years. During that decade, the two townships it served had been transformed by a booming economy from a sleepy, rural, nearly all-White farming region into a bustling, quasisuburban, multicultural area. One result of this economic expansion was a rapid growth in population and a concomitant change in demographics that had a profound effect on the composition of Northern High's student body. In the space of just 10 years, the racial make-up went from 98% White and 2% African-American to 70% White, 22% African-American, and 8% Asian. There had been little change, however, in the composition of Northern staff. Prior to the boom, all 30 teachers had been White. By 1991, there were 85 on the staff, and only two were minority: one was African-American and the other was Asian.

Things began to change 2 years ago when Dr. John DiCaprio became principal. A graduate of Northern nearly 20 years before, he had returned with impressive credentials. A Harvard doctorate and 5 years of administrative experience in the prestigious suburban district of nearby Monroe City had assured the board of his competence, but it was his record at Northern as a student that had assured him the job. He had been student council president, a member of the National Honor Society, captain of the football team, and the only wrestler ever to win a state championship. His elevation to principal was hailed as the return of a favorite son.

That was 2 years ago, and despite the support he enjoyed, his tenure had not been without a few bumps. One of the most sensitive issues, and, in DiCaprio's opinion, one of the most critical, was the racial imbalance between the student body and the teaching staff. When he arrived, Northern Regional had a staff that was 2.5% minority to educate a student body that was 30% minority. DiCaprio had pushed hard for increased minority hiring, but there was a great deal of resistance. A walkout by minority students in spring 1992, triggered in part by this imbalance, had been a wake-up call. Last summer three new teachers had been hired, and two of them were African-American. Minority representation on the staff now stood at 5.7%. Dr. DiCaprio was happy that the district was moving in the right direction.

According to projections by the state economic development authority, this part of the state of New Sussex had been labeled as the state's leading area of growth. Using data provided by the state, the district had estimated that the student population would continue to grow and eventually double within the next 15 years. Of greater significance was the forecast that a sizable number of new students would be African-American and Asian. Dr. DiCaprio had seen in these statistics both a challenge and an opportunity. Increased enrollments translated into increased hiring, and it was through new hiring that Dr. DiCaprio planned to increase the number of minorities on his staff.

DiCaprio's best-laid plans now seemed like pie in the sky. The economic worm had turned! Much of the development in Jefferson County, where Northern's two sending districts were located, had been fueled by growth in two areas. The first was the expansion of high-tech businesses in Monroe City, less than 20 miles away. The second was the increasing number of casinos in Pacific City, less than 30 miles away. The casinos had made shore property along the southern New Sussex coast too expensive for middle-income professionals, and so they had come to Jefferson County seeking affordable housing. With a recession in full swing, casinos went belly up, and the economic boom in Monroe City went bust!

The impact on Northern was immediate. The student population growth curve was, at best, expected to be flat for the next couple of years. Some even foresaw a decrease. To DiCaprio, the handwriting was on the wall; there would have to be a reduction in force (RIF). RIFing was anathema to the teachers' association because it made vulnerable teachers who had gained tenure and, presumably, job security. In deciding whom to let go, the union was adamant that the "last hired, first fired" rule be followed.

For DiCaprio, RIFing was the death knell of his minority hiring program. He had searched far and wide to find the best qualified candidates, and his efforts had not been in vain. The two new African-American teachers had done a great job in their first year at Northern. He could easily think of a dozen tenured teachers he would rather let go. Although he would have dearly loved to violate the "last hired, first fired" rule, DiCaprio knew that to do so would create such a furor that the staff, usually complacent, would most likely rise up and take drastic action, possibly even strike.

It was the first week of April, and the district was required to inform all staff by the end of the month of their employment status for the upcoming year. DiCaprio had just met with the superintendent and received a directive; he would have to eliminate one position. As if that were not bad enough, the decision had been made to effect this reduction by increasing class size in either the math or English department. What a setback! Of the two new African-American teachers hired, one was an English teacher, the other a math teacher. One would have to go! DiCaprio was incensed. He had argued for several other options without success. He knew there had to be another way.

Peter Weiss was finishing up his second year in the social studies department. DiCaprio had frequent conversations with Barbara Meyer, the department head, about him. Peter had been struggling somewhat with his teaching technique and his rapport with students. One sore point was the fact that, although White, he was teaching the African-American history course that had been implemented the year after the student walkout. There was no hard evidence that he was insensitive to the minority students in the class. Complaints came mainly from parents and were philosophical in nature. "How could a White man understand the struggle of African-Americans?" was a query that had been put to him many times.

Beyond this course, DiCaprio and Meyer had some misgivings about Weiss' capability, as evidenced by his mediocre observations. Despite his concerns, DiCaprio believed that every new teacher should be given a fair chance to learn the craft of teaching. He remembered his own first few years in the classroom. His performance had been less than stellar, and he knew that he had needed those 3 years to develop into a good, solid teacher. He had intended to give Weiss the same opportunity. Now, however, as a principal, he had a different set of priorities. He certainly had doubts about Weiss' potential but had been willing to give him one more year. Given the need to reduce his staff by one, his thinking now took a different course.

George Taylor was the African-American English teacher who had been hired the year before. Fresh out of college and single, George had done an outstanding job both in and out of the classroom. He was co-advisor for the African-American Culture Club and had volunteered to run the "We the Students" Committee. DiCaprio had founded this group after the walkout to promote understanding among the races at Northern. He had run it the first year but found that his busy schedule did not permit him to continue in this capacity. When George was hired, he was asked to take over and had done a first-rate job. George also had dual certification in social studies.

If Peter Weiss were not rehired, then George could switch from the English Department to the Social Studies Department. DiCaprio would be able to follow his superintendent's directive to reduce staff in the English or Math Department.

He would be able to keep a gifted minority teacher, have an African-American teaching the course in African-American history, and maintain what meager gains he had made in trying to establish a minority presence on the faculty. Of course, this could be accomplished only if he let Peter Weiss go after his second year; however, this would violate his longstanding belief that teachers should be given at least 3 years to prove themselves.

As he left the office that day, he was, for the first time in a long time, not quite sure what to do. As he rounded the corner, he bumped into Peter Weiss.

"Hey, Dr. DiCaprio, want to see something," Peter said, waving a picture in his hand.

"What have you got there, Peter?" Dr. DiCaprio replied.

"It's a sonogram. My wife and I are going to have twins."

Questions for Discussion

1. What is the fairest decision Dr. DiCaprio could make? The most caring? Are they different? Is what is fair or caring for Peter Weiss the same as what is fair or caring for George Taylor? Are there others who should be considered in trying to determine fairness or caring? If so, who are they? Why those persons?

2. What do you assume would be the consequences to Dr. DiCaprio if he broke the "last hired, first fired rule?" Are there times when rules or laws must be broken to achieve a higher moral level? Do you think this situation is an example of one of those times? Why or why not? Explain.

3. Where do you suppose the "last hired, first fired" rule came from? Could you speculate as to what its original purpose may have been? Do you believe it is a just rule? If you believe the rule is just, do you believe it is absolute? Or are there circumstances under which the rule might be applied differently or not at all? Whose rule is this? Who benefits from the rule in this scenario? Who, in general, would benefit from such a rule?

4. What do you believe is the most moral decision that Dr. DiCaprio could make in this situation? What would you do if you were in his place? Why would you take such action? In this circumstance, are your personal beliefs the same or different from your professional beliefs? Explain.

ACCESS TO KNOWLEDGE

Mackenzie High School, the only high school in Harford County, is a growing comprehensive public high school comprised of Grades 7 through 12 with an enrollment that fluctuates between 2,500 and 3,000 students, of which 55% are minority. The student population varies greatly based on the demographics of the five elementary schools from which students come to enroll in Mackenzie.

The school district in which Mackenzie High School is located is comprised of a tricounty system of one high school with a lower division for Grades 7 through 9 and an upper division that serves students in Grades 10 through 12, and the five elementary schools. All the schools except the high school are located in a geographically contiguous radius of approximately 25 miles.

The elementary feeder schools are quite diverse with regard to socioeconomic status. The two elementary schools that serve the highest socioeconomic community have a combined minority population of less than 20%. On the opposite end of the socioeconomic ladder is Adams Run Elementary School with a minority population of approximately 90%. In the middle are Brown and Jackson Elementary Schools, which serve a low to moderate socio-economic neighborhood with minority populations of about 30% and 40% respectively.

Although the students are diverse in terms of ethnicity, socioeconomic status, and educational need, the faculty of Mackenzie High School is quite homogeneous. Of the 120 professional staff consisting of administrators, counselors, a librarian, and teachers, less than 15% are minority, of which 75% are female.

Mackenzie High School is situated in the center of Harford County, a blue-collar community that is highly active politically. Harford County is populated by citizens with varying ethnicities including African-American, Asian-American, Hispanics, and European-American. The community is nicely balanced in terms of young couples who are just starting out, well-established families, and senior citizens. Harford County is primarily working class with a number of prosperous businesses nearby. The Aerospace Jet Plant, the Harford County Medical Center, and an auto plant that is a subsidiary of General Motors provide the economic base for Harford County. These businesses have provided employment for a large number of residents of Harford County generation after generation.

Harford County, originally a predominantly White, working-class community comprised of citizens from Irish, Polish, and German descent, has changed appreciably over the past decade. Although there has been a significant influx of people from diverse backgrounds, Whites have remained in the majority. Nevertheless, the minority population has had a powerful impact on the town and on Mackenzie High School. This presence has affected the cultural life of Harford County as well as the educational mission of Mackenzie High School.

Ruben and Gabriella Soler moved to Harford County from Puerto Rico approximately a decade ago. The Soler family is typical of the people from diverse populations who gradually migrated to Harford County. Alberto is the youngest of three children. His older brother and sister graduated from Mackenzie High School and obtained employment in the nearby medical center and General Motors plant. However, Alberto's parents wanted a lot more for their youngest son. They were relying on the school to provide the kind of education that Alberto would need to get beyond the factories of Harford County.

When Alberto was small, and from the time he could remember, his parents instilled in him the desire to set his goals high. Moreover, they implored the school to provide programs designed at improving English fluency. They knew that being able to speak and write English was Alberto's ticket out of Harford County, and lack of fluency in English was the main stumbling block that had held back his brother and sister.

Even though Alberto was a very conscientious student, learning did not come easy because his language and his culture were different from the majority of students. As a result, Alberto had been placed in low ability groups since first grade. By the time he entered Mackenzie High School, he had spent approximately 8 years in the lowest functioning group.

Mackenzie High School played an important role in the Harford County community. When the racial make-up of the community began to change, Mackenzie High School attempted to ease the process of assimilation by emphasizing language instruction, offering remedial classes, instituting a more comprehensive vocational educational program, and establishing multicultural courses. Yet, despite all the recent innovations, there has been a growing concern about the future. The White majority, who worked in the factories and surrounding businesses for decades, have become concerned about the future opportunities for their children, especially in view of the recent migration of new residents. They saw the changing economy and increasing population as signs of a future struggle for their children.

Parents of students represented in the minority population feel the same pinch. Both groups want more for their children, and they look to Mackenzie High School to provide the educational preparation children will need for a better tomorrow. They want their children to make better lives for themselves by attending college; consequently, the demand for access to college-bound programs has intensified. In recent years, parents' desires to have their children attend college have been reflected in an increased commitment to academic counseling and college preparatory courses. Moreover, the demand for college-bound classes has focused tremendous attention on the selection process for the placement of students in various programs as well as assignment to tracks.

Issues of access to knowledge and equality of educational opportunity for the minority student population have come to the forefront, and competition has escalated. Minority students make up the majority enrollment in vocational educational classes. Many teachers believe that, on the whole, minority students perform poorly academically because they are below average in intellectual ability. They subscribe to the findings of the research of Jensen, who argued that because average IQ test scores of certain groups (African-Americans and Latinos) are consistently below those of other groups (Whites and Asian-Americans), it is likely that there is a real genetically determined difference in intellectual ability among members of these groups (Jensen, 1969).

The Mackenzie High School community is satisfied with the state of affairs. The staff feels that the school provides an adequate, and in some cases, an excellent education for its students and that it serves Harford County in a fitting manner. The curriculum is balanced so that students can pursue individual interests, and teachers can provide for individual educational needs. The guidance department takes an active role in the process of program selection and placement.

Dr. Patricia Meyerowitz, principal of Mackenzie High School for 8 years, is characterized as a fair-minded, no nonsense, yet quite compassionate, administrator. She exhibits a strong sense of authority, passion, and commitment to the educational mission of Mackenzie High School. During the last 5 years, she has observed a gradual shift in teacher attitude and performance, noticing that many teachers have accepted the idea that minority students cannot be expected to learn at high levels. This notion is reflected in the manner in which students are placed in programs as well as in the quality of instruction offered to them.

Given these circumstances, it is not surprising that Pat Meyerowitz welcomed the concern of Mrs. Gabriella Soler, mother of Alberto Benito Soler, a ninth-grade Latino student who had previously attended Jackson Elementary School where, as indicated earlier, he had been placed in low-functioning groups for most of his educational life. Alberto entered Mackenzie High School in seventh grade where he continued in the lowest functioning group.

Mrs. Soler was mindful of the attitudes of staff at Mackenzie High School. She had had numerous meetings with the guidance counselor during the past 2 years and based on her past experiences, she had little doubt that minority students were not treated fairly at Mackenzie High School; moreover, Mrs. Soler had grown to distrust the judgment of Alberto's teachers. Despite unwavering effort and pleading to have her son placed in a higher group, Alberto spent 2 years in classes that did little to meet his interests or his educational needs.

Now, Alberto is preparing to enter the upper division of Mackenzie High School. His ambition is to go to college; therefore, he wants to be placed in the college-bound program. Mrs. Soler has determined that Alberto has not been treated fairly by the chairperson of the guidance division, Maryanne Polkalsky, because she has denied him access to the college-bound program.

Maryanne Polkalsky, a pillar of the community, is widely known in Harford County. It seems as though she has been at Mackenzie High School forever. She had advised most of the students' parents and, throughout the years, has assigned many working-class and poorer students into nonacademic tracks. She is powerful and uses this power masterfully to maintain control. Ms. Polkalsky is accustomed to being bombarded by parents and students, and uses the authority of her position to skillfully maneuver students into programs where she feels they are suited. Her decisions have made it generally impossible for minority students to escape a lifetime of work in the factories that surround Harford County.

In recent years, resentment has mounted because many of the minority students and their parents have been denied access to an equal educational opportunity, and they have openly discussed Maryanne Polkalsky's misuse and abuse of power and authority. As judge and jury, Maryanne decided that Alberto would not do well in the college-bound track and should register for the vocational program.

Mrs. Soler feels that Mrs. Polkalsky has no right to thwart Alberto's dream of going to college when most of the nonminority students are given a fair chance to prepare for college by their placement in the college-bound program. Furthermore, Mrs. Soler has observed that a disproportionate number of Latino and African-American students are enrolled in vocational education courses. In fact, Mrs. Soler is convinced that Mrs. Polkalsky's treatment of Alberto is based on prejudice, and that this is but one example of the treatment of minority students at Mackenzie High School. She is cognizant that most of the minority students are advised to join the work force, to apply for apprenticeship programs, or join the armed services. Few, if any, are recommended for college.

Mrs. Soler is convinced that minority students do not achieve at high levels at Mackenzie High School because the school culture favors the White majority, which places minority students from other backgrounds and cultures at a serious disadvantage. Teachers do not create a democratic environment in their classrooms, nor do they exhibit attitudes of caring and concern. Alberto has a fundamental right to the same opportunity afforded to White students, and Mrs. Soler is demanding that her son be given equal access to knowledge and the same educational opportunity that nonminority students receive so that Alberto can acquire the background, skills, and knowledge necessary to fulfill his dream of going to college after high school.

Principal Meyerowitz conveyed Mrs. Soler's sentiments to Maryanne Polkalsky. Maryanne assured Dr. Meyerowitz that her decision was made in Alberto's best interests. Alberto was recommended for the vocational education program based on his record of prior academic achievement including standardized test results and recommendations from his teachers. An objective evaluation revealed that Alberto was in the lower quartile of his class, and Maryanne was confident that he did not possess the aptitude and the language development required to do well in college.

Moreover, she emphasized that in light of the financial burden of college, it would be an injustice to mislead Alberto and his family. She felt it was her professional duty to guide Alberto toward an attainable goal, namely joining the workforce after graduating from high school. Pat Meyerowitz did not doubt Maryanne's sincerity or her good will. Nor did she think for one moment that Maryanne's decision was in Alberto's best interests.

As an educator, Maryanne Polkalsky is in the position of deciding what path Alberto's life will take. She is considered an expert in her field. This is a job that she has done for years, and as far as many people are concerned, she has done it well. On the other hand, Pat Meyerowitz, as principal, is the instructional leader of the school. She recognizes that Maryanne is strongly influenced by past practices that have had an unsympathetic outcome on minority students.

Is Alberto entitled equal access to good instruction and equality of opportunity so that he can gain the skills and knowledge necessary to attain his goal? What should Dr. Meyerowitz do?

Questions for Discussion

1. One could argue that because Alberto had been tracked into low ability groups since first grade, he had received an inequitable education from the beginning and, thus, was not given the preparation he needed to compete for a college preparatory program. Do you agree with this statement? Assuming it is true, does the school have a moral obligation to right this situation? If so, how?

2. Is tracking just? Is tracking in the best interests of students in general? Any students? Are there types or methods of tracking that are more fair than others? If so, what are they? If not, why not?

3. What are the benefits of tracking? What are the detriments? Is tracking mostly an economic issue? If so, in what ways? If not, why not? What else needs to be considered in educating students? Who makes the rules about tracking and to what purpose?

4. What would a caring administrator do in this situation? A caring guidance director?

5. What is your view of the ethics of tracking from a professional point of view? From a personal point of view?

6. In this particular scenario, do you agree with Pat or Maryanne? Explain your reasoning. If you were Pat, what would you do to make an ethical decision? If you were Maryanne, how would you handle this situation in the most ethical manner?

7. What would you tell the Solers? If you really believed that Alberto could not make it through a college preparatory program, would you tell him? Do you believe that Alberto has a right to fail? Do Maryanne or Pat have a responsibility to protect Alberto from failure? If so, what course of action might they take? If not, why not? Should all students, regardless of academic success, be permitted to take whatever courses they wish? Why or why not? If not, how does one decide where to draw the line?

III

TEACHING AS SCHOLARLY WORK

Part III is meant to assist anyone who might be teaching or who wants to teach ethics to educators. We begin by focusing on instructors, and in this particular case, on ourselves as professors of ethics in educational leadership. We take the reader on a reflective journey. During the journey, we describe how we thought through our own personal and professional codes of ethics and we reflect on the critical incidents in our lives that shaped our teaching. This self-reflective process helped us to determine what we privileged in our classroooms. This section also deals with our approaches to teaching ethics, the issues we faced, the theoretical underpinnings behind our pedagogy, and the value of ethics in educational leadership programs.

In this section of the book, we attempt to provide one model to illustrate the concept of scholarly teaching that was introduced by Boyer (1990), in the Carnegie Foundation's report, *Scholarship Reconsidered: Priorities of the Professoriate*. Through a form of self-reflection and peer review that we developed during a 9-year period, we began to define our teaching of ethics as scholarly work. In fact, some of our published writings on ethics have sections in them where we speak of our pedagogy and what we have learned through self-reflection and peer review. This concept of teaching as scholarly work continues to be recommended by Shulman (1997) and by Hutchings (1998) of The Carnegie Foundation for the Advancement of Teaching. It is a concept that we take seriously.

This part of the book also discusses our experiences in teaching ethics to diverse educational leaders. It explains how we have come to believe that this training is needed for educational leaders, especially in our changing society, as we enter the next millennium.

8

Ethics, Ourselves, and Our Pedagogy

We know precious little about how professors balance the academic ideal of rigorous scholarship with what might be called a core pastoral concern to nurture and challenge the ethical values and world view of their students. Furthermore, we know precious little about the attitudes, beliefs, and personal journeys of educators practicing in educational administration programs.

—Starratt (1994b, p. 100)

Even though scholars may recognize the importance of ethics for educational leaders, they have not yet been able to resolve how this subject can be or should be taught. Additionally, little research has been conducted on this question (Beck & Murphy, 1994a). This chapter is meant to encourage self-reflection on the part of instructors. It is also intended to serve as a rubric to discuss our methods of teaching ethics and how this approach is carried out with diverse students.

THE TEACHING OF ETHICS: OUR PERSPECTIVE

In this secular age, with all of the problems that confront us, we think it is extremely important for those of us who carry out instruction in ethics to have a sense of who we are and what we believe in personally and professionally. In our case, we realized inasmuch as we ask our students to embark on difficult soul-searching assignments, such as developing their own personal and professional codes, then it is important that we do the same. Furthermore, as two professors who taught basically the same content in an ethics course in different academic years to similar educational administration doctoral cohort groups, we felt that such explorations might have profound effects, enabling us to compare and contrast how we teach such a course and why we choose to teach it in the ways we do.

We tend to believe what Witherell and Noddings (1991) have written: "To educate is to take seriously both the quest for life's meaning and the meaning of individual lives" (p. 3). We have been affected by the works of Belenky, Clinchy, Goldberger, and Tarule (1986); Beck (1994); Gilligan (1982); Gilligan, Ward, and Taylor (1988); Maher and Tetreault (1994); Noddings (1984, 1992); Shapiro and Smith-Rosenberg (1989); and others who have stressed the importance of developing a voice and have come to realize that life stories and personal experiences can be powerful. Such stories can help to determine who we are today both personally and professionally.

We have also been affected by the work of Bakhtin (1981), Freire (1970), Kohlberg (1981), Purpel (1989), and others in their quest for dialogue and knowledge of "self" in relation to others. Difficult dialogue leading to self-disclosure can be a most trying process, but it can also assist us in making our once hidden ethical codes explicit. Furthermore, it can take what might be deemed a selfish process of focusing on the "self" and use it as a way to serve and care for others by helping them find their voices and their values.

Before we discuss our course and its pedagogical implications in more detail, we would like to spend a little time providing an overview of our backgrounds and a few critical incidents that shaped our lives. After considerable reflection, we believe that these stories have led to the development of both our personal and professional ethical codes. We also believe that such self-disclosures are needed to assist us in better understanding our pedagogical approaches and how we affect our students (Stefkovich & Shapiro, 1994).

THE PROFESSORS' STORIES

On the surface, the two of us seem to be somewhat similar. We are both White females; we are both from the northeastern seaboard; we both have doctoral degrees in educational administration from Ivy League institutions; and we are both middle class and about the same age. However, that is as far as our similarities go.

In fact, we are very different individuals. Part of the difference is explained in our education and professional preparation, but this formal education and its socialization does not tell enough. Our stories and the critical incidents within them have tended to shape who we are. We have chosen parts of our lives that we feel have had an impact on how we came to approach the same ethics course in different ways. Rather than pretend that we came to the course with open minds, we think it is important to indicate some of the experiences and perspectives that we brought with us.

Joan's Story

When I reflect on my own personal ethical code, I know that I have been shaped by my religious roots as a Jew, and by the area where I grew up, in the northeastern part of the United States, which stressed the Puritan work ethic and a form of Social Darwinism in which individual hard work and competition were thought to be healthy values. The notion seemed clear at that time, growing up as a middle-class child in Connecticut, that we all had opportunity, if only we worked hard.

However, I know that my code of values and ethics has been deeply shaped by the years I spent in college—a time when the civil rights movement was growing. While in college, I gave considerable thought to the concept of discrimination, and I remember many a holiday having verbal battles with my parents about the civil rights movement and civil disobedience. In fact, soon after graduation, during my honeymoon, my 18-year-old British brother-in-law accompanied my husband and me singing peace and civil rights songs. The three of us were so keen that we were the only Whites attending a rally in Washington, DC at which Martin Luther King spoke. My family and friends thought that I had had a very strange honeymoon indeed.

My ethical code was also shaped by teaching British history in London, England, for a few years to working-class children who had little chance to advance because they had not passed the 11 + exam, an exam that determined if they were university material or not at the tender age of 11 or so. I taught in a secondary modern all-girls' school composed of students who were either from working-class White Anglo-Saxon families or from working-class families of color from diverse Commonwealth countries. The options for students in this school generally were to become hairdressers, shop assistants, or at best secretaries in the high road nearby. Even when we "went comprehensive," under the Labor government, a tracking system prohibited my students from having opportunities to move toward higher education. In England's secondary schools, I saw injustices primarily based on the intersection of social class with race, ethnicity, or both.

Some years later, I returned to the United Kingdom to spend a postdoctoral year at the University of London's Institute of Education. There I was exposed to the rich tradition of the philosophy of education that seemed to permeate all of education. The philosophical works of Peters (1973) and Hirst (1974), for example, were held in high regard. Peters and Hirst were able to combine the liberal tradition of justice with more of an emotional and caring quality. Their respect for both the cognitive and affective domains had an effect on me.

Most importantly, beyond the formal classroom, during the 4 years I lived in the United Kingdom, I was impressed with British society's ability to combine socialism with the "noblesse oblige" spirit that still existed from the Middle Ages. The government provided national health care, generous university grants for poor students, and welfare benefits that did not stigmatize people. Unlike many Americans, schooled in Social Darwinism, I began to feel that society had an obligation to look after its people in appropriate ways, if at all possible, from the cradle to the grave.

Thus far in my life, my consciousness had been raised in the areas of religion, race, and social class, but it took a critical incident for me to focus on the category of gender discrimination. It was Uncle Max's funeral that was the turning point for me in the category of gender.

Uncle Max's funeral took place in the northern part of England, in which a very fundamentalist sect of Jews lived. When my husband and I arrived at Uncle Max's home, the women were moaning and wailing around a hearse that waited outside the door. This seemed strange to me because Uncle Max was well into his 80s and had not suffered unduly before his death. With my husband, I went to the burial grounds for the ceremony. At the grounds, much to my surprise, I turned out to be the only woman present and was told not to leave the car. Apparently, women were not allowed on the burial grounds lest they "sully the soil."

This was a painful experience for me. I had only recently buried my father, in the conservative Jewish tradition, and my mother, sister, and I had been free to mourn publicly and on the cemetery grounds. It seemed to me that the humiliation for women continued that day when the Rabbi told Auntie Minnie, Uncle Max's wife of 45 years, that she missed an excellent speech he had given on behalf of her husband on the burial grounds. All the women around me seemed to accept, without comment, what I perceived to be an insult, but I was never the same. Gender became an overriding category of difference and discrimination in my life, making me into a feminist.

Seven years of co-directing a women's studies program at the University of Pennsylvania continued to raise my consciousness toward injustices—not just in the area of sexism but in the realms of race, ethnicity, social class, sexual orientation, and disability. In reflecting on patriarchy, power, and hierarchy, I began to realize the great impact of society and how it can manage to keep diverse groups in their place. Dealing with issues of oppression, victimization, and difference, I began to understand how groups have been socially constructed by those in power and the effect of that construction on individuals within the group. Collectivity, social responsibility, and care of others were concepts that struck a chord with me, moving me away from "rugged individualism" and Social Darwinism. Thanks to studying feminist scholarship, I began to question abstract justice, rights, and law.

My background, the numerous critical incidents in my life, the years I spent in England and in the area of women's studies led me to focus heavily on the underdog in society. I seem to care deeply about injustices of all kinds. I constantly ask: Who has been omitted? Whose voice is missing? Whose ethical values am I privileging? Whose ethical values is society privileging? I often think about the good of the whole community as well as the good of different groups within the community.

However, my code of ethics, I now realize, is not simplistic. On issues related to one's body and one's life, I am very much committed to individual liberty and privacy. Thus, in all cases, I do not disdain the rights of the individual. I am, then, a situational ethicist, who leans toward a belief in our need to have a moral commitment beyond self toward those less fortunate and those who are different from ourselves—toward the concept of social responsibility.

Privilege

Leaders need to be deeply reflective, actively thoughtful, and dramatically explicit about their core values and beliefs. (Bolman & Deal, 1991, p. 449)

Initially, I tried to make certain that the graduate students in this ethics course had some introduction to traditional ethics. I provided an overview of the major Western thinkers in the field, focusing on utilitarianism, consequentialist and nonconsequentialist theory, and basic liberal tenets of Western philosophy based on individual rights.

The language of rights was further discussed as we sorted out moral dilemmas raised by Strike, Haller, and Soltis (1988), and I asked the students to use the step-by-step process advocated in their book. This process moved from the presentation of a case, to the establishment of the dispute, to the setting forth of different arguments, and finally to the resolving of the dilemma. Although this framework was used, I spent considerable time critiquing the arguments put forth in this ethics book. It seemed to me important for students to see that a basic text was not the gospel and that there were other approaches that could be used to answer the dilemmas discussed in the book. In many ways, I sought to raise questions that would challenge the liberal democratic philosophy espoused in this text.

Although I did not leave out the language of rights, justice, and law, I had my students listen to other voices and turn to the language of critique and possibilities as well as the language of care, concern, and connectedness over time. These forms of ethics are presented by alternative ethicists.

In particular, to introduce the students to alternative forms of ethics, I spent considerable time in class focusing on the work of Purpel. In his book, *The Moral and Spiritual Crisis in Education*, Purpel (1989) described a complex form of ethics that made an excellent bridge from traditional to nontraditional ethics. Purpel himself indicated that he borrowed from "two ancient traditions, the Socratic and the Prophetic and two theological movements: Liberation Theology and Creation Theology" (p. xi). This mix enabled students to move from liberal democratic ethics focused on law and justice to areas of social justice and compassion.

Throughout his work, Purpel challenges us to deal with the complexities and the contradictions of the modern world and leave behind any simplistic notions of right and wrong or good and bad. He introduces important paradoxes, and, in so doing, highlights areas of miscommunication that frequently lead to misunderstandings. These paradoxes include concepts of control–democracy, individual-ity–community, worth–achievement, equality–competition, and compassion–sen-timentality. These paradoxes are maintained by society and they trickle down to our schools. Although he does not classify himself as a critical theorist, he does set the stage for those who challenge the current system, and he makes us reflect upon the important concepts of democracy, social justice, privilege, and power as they relate to schooling. Through Purpel's work, I was able to turn to the writings of critical theorists as I felt that the class and I were ready to discuss the writings of Giroux (1991, 1994) who not only challenged the system, but also offered promise through the concept of "the language of possibilities."

Under the concept of the language of possibilities, a number of critical theo-rists recommend activism and social change. Collective effort, learning through service, and local involvement—what Welch (1991) might call working toward solidarity within one's own community—are parts of the message. In many ways, Purpel, as well as the critical theorists, moves away from the remote, neutral, seemingly objective discussion of rights, law, and justice that tend to be ethical ar-guments of the traditional liberal democracies and toward the inclusion of feeling, emotion, and compassion in ethics.

Other nontraditional education ethicists I privileged when I taught the course were feminist ethicists. To illustrate feminist ethics, I turned primarily to the works of Gilligan (1982; Gilligan, Ward, & Taylor, 1988) and also to a study (Shapiro & Smith-Rosenberg, 1989) carried out when my colleague, Carroll Smith-Rosenberg, and I taught a women's studies ethics course. Prior to examin-ing the works of feminist ethicists—in particular, Gilligan—I spent time discuss-ing the writings of Kohlberg. I discussed Kohlberg's groundbreaking work based on an analysis of 84 children's (boys') responses to moral dilemmas over a 20-year period and his development of six stages of moral development.

Although I admire Kohlberg's work, I tended to use his scholarship as a way to introduce Gilligan and her inclusion of girls into the moral development stage the-ory. I then turned to Gilligan as a scholar who was able to critique Kohlberg's stage theory. In so doing, she revealed responses, not taken into account by Kohlberg. She introduced us to the voice of concern, connectedness, relatedness over time, and caring. She felt this voice to be important and yet, in Kohlberg's stage theory, it was invisible—hence, many girls and boys who were caring young people often received low scores using his stages.

Gilligan's critique and the work of scholars such as Noddings (1984, 1992), Belenky, Clinchy, Goldberger, and Tarule (1986), and others made me aware that all voices need not be categorized in traditional ethical ways focusing on justice, law, and rights. There are indeed other voices that are important in this society and should be valued. My own experiences in the 3 years I taught ethics to under-graduates with Carroll Smith-Rosenberg led me to believe that what Gilligan, Noddings, and others had written had meaning.

Furthermore, in Shapiro and Smith-Rosenberg (1989), we discovered in our own classes many illustrations of alternative ethical thinking. We were able to give examples of students' approaches to solving moral dilemmas through their writings in journals that showed how powerful the voice of care, concern, and connectedness was within our women's studies classroom.

On reflection, then, it seems clear to me that I tended to privilege the voice of critique and possibilities and the voice of care, concern, and connectedness over the voice of abstract rights, law, and justice. Nevertheless, it also became clear that although the majority of graduate students could hear all of these voices, some could not. This proved to be somewhat disappointing. However, judging from the course evaluations, the journal entries, the personal and professional codes, the ethical dilemmas, and the comments in and out of class, overall, I noted that most of the graduate students were able to at least stand back and reflect on the concepts of the "rugged individual," individual rights, and abstract justice that previously many of them accepted, without question, as the best principles for our current society.

Jackie's Story

My own values and ethical code have evolved through the years. I was raised in a Catholic working-class family in a rural community in western Pennsylvania. It was here that I learned the importance of honesty, respect for others, and hard work. Mine was the first generation in that town that went to college, and my family viewed an education as the most important goal that one could achieve—both as an end in itself and as a way up and out of a tough life.

In the 1920s, the community where I grew up had been a bustling coal town, but the Great Depression hit hard and the mines closed. Most of the men in the town—those of my parents' generation—turned to labor jobs in neighboring steel mills while their wives stayed at home raising the children. The men of my generation—if not college bound—took on the hard and often dangerous life of an iron worker. The women married young and became hairdressers or, if they were lucky enough to be educated, teachers.

There was a definite pecking order in this town. Those who had been fortunate enough to immigrate first, the English and the Welsh, owned farms with large houses and a great deal of land. The Irish came next and often had jobs working for the township. At the bottom of this ladder were those who carried with them the stigma of long, funny last names—the Italians and the eastern Europeans. These were the majority and I was one of them.

"You have really got to get that name changed," the town pharmacist said to an 11-year-old me as he stumbled over the name while filling my prescription. "Perhaps you will marry someone with a shorter last name." That was the first time that I remember the sting of discrimination. It always struck me as odd that my grandmother—who came from Czechoslovakia in 1916, played the piano, spoke five languages, and raised seven children alone after her young husband was killed in a mine cave-in—was somehow inferior because she carried the badge of a long last name. And I also shared that disdain of others—and that limitation—because of my name and my ethnicity.

This was only one of a number of similar childhood incidents, but it remains most vivid in my mind because it was the first time that I came head to head with the painful realization that I might be limited because of something I could not help—because of who I was. Even at eleven, I realized that to be as good as other people, I would need to do more than change my name, I would need to deny my identity, my culture, my background, and my family.

This denial of self was something that I have never been prepared to do—either then or now, decades later. But I always carried that memory with me and vowed that I would never, at least intentionally, impose that pain or stigma on any other human being. It was not until I attended college in the late 1960s that I was exposed to people of other races and other cultures and, after hearing their stories, realized how insignificant my pain must have been compared to that of so many others.

Thus, a respect for human dignity and a focus on the worth of each person as a unique individual has always been an important value for me. This value began early on, but took shape during my college years. I majored in psychology at a time and at a university where a strong liberal arts education was stressed. And quite by accident, I happened to be at one of the few universities in this country that approaches psychology from the European tradition of existentialism. So, instead of running rats in mazes, I studied Kant and Sartre and pondered the meaning of existence, something that, at the time, seemed quite exotic for a first generation college-educated female from a blue-color background. Nonetheless, this experience greatly influenced my present view of life as well as my approach to teaching.

Formal education as a personally enriching experience, as a key to open doors of opportunity, and as a compensation to counter perceived shortcomings (with regards to ethnicity and gender) has always figured largely in my life. I earned a masters' degree in counseling immediately after undergraduate school and, after some 13 years of working in public schools and in state bureaucracy, I quit what my family perceived as a "good" (meaning "stable") job to attend graduate school full time. During the next 7 years, I completed a doctorate in educational administration as well as a law degree.

Each of these educational experiences taught me important lessons and each shaped my values in different ways. It was through my counseling program that I learned the meaning of empathy, a key concept in the profession. "It's not the same as sympathy," I remember my professors saying. "It's being able to put yourself in someone else's shoes, to feel as they feel." It is no wonder that today one of my favorite contemporary philosophers is John Rawls, who believes that a just outcome is one that a person would arrive at having no idea which role he or she played in any given moral dilemma.

As part of my doctoral program in educational administration, I took an elective course with Kohlberg and learned about the longitudinal studies that gave rise to his theory of moral development. It was here also that I was first exposed to the works of Gilligan. It was in this program that I wrote a doctoral dissertation on students' privacy rights and, in my first school law class, began to understand both the limitations and the power of the law in remedying social inequities. I learned about issues of equity and inequity and about the obligations that we as educated people have to right these wrongs.

At law school, I learned about justice or at least what I have come to realize as a man-made version of justice. I took courses with Lani Guinier and worked as her graduate student studying the Voting Rights Act and pondering the mechanisms of our democratic system. It was also in law school where I began to realize that my long-held beliefs in individual rights could come into conflict with my concerns about equity. This intersection of civil liberties and civil rights continues to influence my teaching, my research, and my personal and professional values. I see the conflict between the two as a source of concern, as a mystery yet to be solved.

Although I have alluded to gender, I mention it this late in my story because I never perceived it as an influential or limiting factor in my early years. I was the older of two children—3 ½ years older than my brother—and, in many ways, was my father's first "son." Thus, expectations for me, as for all first children, were high. I often teased my parents saying that they wanted a son so badly they named me "Jack," something that my mother—who chose my very feminine first name (Jacqueline) and who spent a great deal of her 20s searching out frilly dresses for me and curling my straight hair—denied vehemently.

The upshot of this juxtaposition between Jack and Jacqueline, between the identity of first-born "son" and Shirley Templesque daughter, was that I grew up seeing myself as androgynous. Obviously, I was female, but I never viewed it as a limitation. I felt competent and respected, both at home and at school. When I read about male heroes, I always identified with the main character. When I watched my favorite swashbuckler movies—Robin Hood and Captain Blood—I was Robin Hood as much as Maid Marian. I was Errol Flynn as much as Olivia de Havilland. To me, neither role seemed inferior; they were instead, complementary.

My parents' attitudes about hard work and education as a way to improve social class influenced me deeply. These aspirations affected me no less, and possibly more, than my brother because I was the first born and also more interested in academics. It was only as I grew older and entered the work force that I saw my gender as a limiting factor. It was with some dismay, and a great deal of incredulity, that I realized an individual's worth could be diminished and opportunities determined solely because of x and y chromosomes.

Thus, I enter the teaching of ethics coming from a background in psychology and law that stresses a traditional, liberal democratic philosophy combined with values that have shaped my thinking. The latter include, above all, a respect for each individual's worth and contribution, a desire for justice, fairness, and equity, and a high regard for the ability to empathize. How these values are translated into my teaching is probably best reflected in what I privilege, that is, what I emphasize in the classroom, just as Joan's values influence what she privileges.

Privilege

> Ethical education is not a simple training in the predisposition to be ethical, the lessons of which, once learned guarantee an ethical adulthood. Ethical education is lifelong education. It takes place simultaneously with our efforts to be human. (Starratt, 1994a, p. 135)

I began my class much as Joan had with an overview of traditional ethics and an exploration of the concepts of utilitarianism as well as consequentialist and nonconsequentialist theories. In the beginning, my students were confused when we discussed traditional ethics; they asked for more—more readings, more clarification, more discussion. After all, we had condensed the whole of Western philosophy into one or two short lessons. To compensate for what I saw as an overly brief introduction and to make sure that the students would feel grounded in the traditional approach, I stressed these theories throughout my teaching and tried to reinforce their significance in relation to the more modern, less traditional, works of Gilligan, Foster, and Purpel.

I also used several dilemmas set forth by Strike, Haller, and Soltis (1988) as a starting point for discussion. Unlike Joan, I did not follow the step-by-step process set forth in the text, but instead made up my own questions. These inquiries generally focused on issues of "What does all this mean?" and "What does it mean to you, personally?" This approach to ethics is advocated by Starratt (1994a) and articulated in his book, *Building an Ethical School.*

Although Strike et al. come from the same type of liberal democratic tradition that I espouse, I did not always agree with their analysis or with the way the dilemma was constructed. This was particularly true with respect to one situation that involved a principal stopping by a bar on the way home from a meeting only to find his prim English teacher working there as a topless dancer to support her sick mother. The principal was not even sure that it was she until the teacher came up to him later to talk, still dressed in her "costume," a sequined G-string.

The overall situation seems conceivable, but this type of "Marian the Librarian" story in which a woman sheds her conservative clothing and turns into a vamp, although interesting, struck me as lacking verisimilitude. And, as a number of students in my class pointed out, Strike neglected to broach the ethical issue of what the principal was doing in a topless bar. If there were an ethical problem here, was not the principal as ethically bound as the dancer? Would the situation have been different if the principal had been a woman and the teacher a man?

Granted, the authors may have left these points out on purpose to stimulate discussion. If so, the strategy worked.

In spite of the fact that my approach, and my analysis, often differed from that of Strike and his associates, I was fascinated with many of the dilemmas they presented because they were very close to legal cases that I had taught in my school law class. For instance, one such scenario involved a teacher writing a letter, to the local press, that criticized the school. "That's the Pickering case," I thought—or at least a modified version of it. Indeed, Strike pointed out that ethical problems and legal problems are often the same. When I first read this statement, it did not quite ring true to me, but I was not sure why. However, after thinking long and hard, I have come to at least a tentative solution.

Court opinions often talk about justice, a concept that Kohlberg (1981) characterizes as a higher stage of moral development. Indeed, the symbol for the legal system is a blindfolded woman holding evenly balanced scales. Consequently, legal opinions handed down by the courts are considered to be just decisions. This interpretation makes sense to me in relation to Strike's statement. As a lawyer as well as an educator, I believe in the power of the law and witness its justice. I see the good that has come from important legal decisions, such as *Brown v. Board of Education,* the United States Supreme Court's famous school desegregation decision, and Brown's progeny, as well as subsequent federal legislation, which secured the rights of women, linguistic minorities, and persons with disabilities.

However, as Starratt (1994c) pointed out, "What happens when the law is wrong?" Indeed, the law is sometimes wrong, as evidenced by the Jim Crow laws requiring racial segregation and the *Plessy v. Ferguson* (1896) decision that upheld the notion that separate is equal. Moreover, sometimes the law is left open for considerable interpretation and consequently leaves government officials (e.g., public school administrators) with a great deal of discretion in carrying out legal mandates. Therefore, I agree with Starratt, and ask a related question: "What happens when the law does not go far enough?"

This last question is one that I posed to the second ethics class I taught in one of their final lessons. Here, I diverted from Joan's original syllabus and added the facts only (not the legal analysis) of *Cornfield v. Consolidated School District No. 230* (1993), a court opinion that I often include in my legal research. This case involved a total nude strip search of a male high school student for drugs. I gave my class the following instructions: "Here are the facts of a recent court decision. Assume the actions the school officials took were legal. (The federal appeals court for the seventh circuit said they were legal in that jurisdiction.) Are they ethical? And, given similar circumstances, how would you act if you were the school administrator?"

Because this exercise was presented late in the course, I was able to use it as a vehicle to encourage the students to explore traditional conceptions of justice as well as to apply nontraditional views such as feminist and critical theory. Unlike Joan, I spent little time lecturing on critical theory. Although I assigned the same chapters in Purpel's and Foster's books that Joan did, I only used them as starting points for discussion of students' personal and professional codes and ultimately for analysis of the strip search case.

Conversely, I spent a good deal of time on Gilligan's work, but I approached it only after an extensive overview of Kohlberg's theory and his stages of moral development. Probably because of my earlier training in psychology, I liked the idea of developmental stages. Also, as I mentioned before, I had taken a course with Kohlberg and have always respected his work. Thus, I presented his theory in some detail, noting that his research was seriously called into question as it relates to women because his sample consisted only of men. I also spent considerable time encouraging my class to discuss caring as part of ethics and how this concepts fits with notions of justice.

OUR PEDAGOGY AND THE ISSUES WE FACE

Our teaching of ethics involves a 7-week course required for the doctoral cohort in our educational administration program. Although we believe that ethics may be taught effectively in many ways, we have found that dealing with the issues we have come to face—concerns about diversity, prior preparation, and an ever-evolving view of ethics as a process requiring self-reflection—is handled more easily when adequate time is allotted. Recognizing that the teaching of ethics can be difficult, it is our desire to share our experiences with others so they might learn from both our successes and limitations. It is in this spirit that we describe our pedagogy and the particular issues we faced in teaching ethics.

Pedagogy

Although Joan privileges the ethic of care and critique and Jackie privileges the ethic of justice, our approaches to pedagogy are remarkably similar. We envision our instruction to be reflective, process-oriented, and constructivist in that we encourage students not to memorize class notes and ethical codes, but to reflect on their own experiences and through them derive meaning from what they have learned. Our aim, then, is to empower our students and/or practitioners so that they in turn will empower others.

We use basically the same readings and take into account diverse perspectives of ethics through the use of the paradigms of justice, caring, critique, and, more recently, the professional model. We employ a variety of teaching approaches including lectures, class discussions, and small group activities.

We expect students to keep personal journals as an aid in helping them to reflect on their experiences. They are also required to write a moral dilemma of their own, to provide an analysis based on what they had learned, and to present their dilemmas and analyses to the class. We encourage students to compare and contrast written ethical codes, both personal and professional, and talk about the similarities they shared as well as the differences. As we have taught this course, we have also encountered challenges, issues that needed to be addressed before we could proceed.

Diversity as a Strength and a Challenge

During the period from 1990 to 1999, we taught more than 150 graduate students as part of their doctoral cohort requirement. Probably most striking about our students is their diversity. Ours is an urban university and, likely because of its location, has been fortunate in attracting students from a variety of racial and ethnic backgrounds. But the students in our ethics classes also have been diverse in many other ways.

Some students came from Philadelphia, the location of our university and the fifth largest city in the United States; others came from smaller Pennsylvania cities such as Harrisburg and Scranton. Some came from other states such as New Jersey, Delaware, and Maryland. Some students commuted from very rural areas, whereas others lived in wealthy suburbs. In one class, we had a woman from Trinidad, a man from Ethiopia, a relocated New Yorker, and a student born and raised in Pennsylvania Dutch country (home of the state's substantial Amish and Mennonite populations).

Although mostly Christian or Jewish, our students represented a variety of factions within these religions. These factions, we thought, tended to influence their personal and professional codes that, more often than not, sounded like some version of the Ten Commandments. For instance, some students belonged to Philadelphia's Black Baptist churches. Others were White Christian fundamentalists from a Bible Belt part of our state. We taught Jewish students, a Catholic nun, persons from a wide variety of Protestant religions, and people who never mentioned religion as part of their identity.

Our students ranged in age from the mid-20s to almost 60, and their professional experiences were often just as diverse. As might be expected, we had our share of public school teachers or administrators; however, others did not necessarily fit the mold of what might be expected in a doctoral program in educational administration. Some came from business. Others worked in higher education institutions. There were counselors, psychologists, biologists, and English and physics teachers. And, just as we, the professors, came to this experience with certain predilections, so did our students. It was through our pedagogy that both we and our students came to understand our values and the critical incidents in our lives that shaped them.

We believe this quality of diversity accounts for the classes' greatest strength in that it enables different perspectives on ethical issues to be discussed. It also presents the greatest challenges to us as teachers because this diversity proved to be a complex phenomenon not easily defined nor easily handled. As we taught our classes, it became readily apparent that diversity was not so obvious.

We could never really resolve the differences among our students. Nor should we. What we could do, though, was employ strategies that would draw students out and force them to reflect on their own ethical codes as well as the perspectives of others in the class.

In teaching this course, we also had to be very careful to guard against stereotypes of any kind, not just the most obvious—along for example race and gender lines—but also the more subtle stereotypes based on religion, culture, geographical location, profession, and previous training. And we not only had to check ourselves, but also our students, always challenging preconceived assumptions and ingrained notions. Dealing with diverse cultures, backgrounds, and opinions meant that we, as teachers, had to constantly be alert to what was happening in our classes.

As we taught this course, we found ourselves grappling with clashes of culture regarding diverse student populations and ultimately acting as translators for our students, crossing borders of gender, race, social class, and other categories of difference to make meanings of others' values, morals, and ethical codes. Through this process, we, too, benefitted, growing—as teachers and as human beings—from these experiences.

These strengths of diversity in our classrooms, the challenges diversity has brought, and how we met these challenges in our pedagogy reinforce our earlier discussions on privilege and pedagogy and our acceptance that there can be no "one best model" for the teaching of ethics.

Prior Preparation in Ethics

In addition to these aspects of diversity that provided us with many challenges, another important difficulty that we faced in our teaching, and one related to diversity, was that most of our students had little or no background in ethics. Consequently, these students were often not quite sure what was expected of them; ethics was very different from the "typical" educational administration courses to which they were accustomed.

In some of our classes, there were also a few students who represented the other end of this spectrum in that they had been exposed to numerous ethics courses, sometimes as a byproduct of religious training. However, they, too, faced ambiguity when dealing with our class because, for the most part, their training had been in the liberal democratic tradition as well as the Judeo–Christian tradition.

The first group, the majority, reacted to this ambiguity by seeking more structure. For instance, when asked to write a personal code, there were always questions as to what this would entail and, in each of our classes, someone inevitably asked if we could provide a sample personal ethical code as a model. On the other hand, the few who had had ethics training generally seemed comfortable with this task. For them, the challenge was to broaden and possibly shake preconceived notions of "truth."

In the end, as students grew accustomed to this way of thinking and more comfortable with the introspection so critical in this process, they began to see the merit in what had first seemed like a most unusual classroom experience. It was at this point that many of our students expressed appreciation for this opportunity, some wishing that there had been more time.

In her journal, one student nicely summed up this sentiment by reflecting upon her own experiences as well as the diversity she encountered:

> (A) course such as this, with the participants we have in class, would be beneficial to everyone. How many of us get the opportunity to really "hear" the beliefs and thoughts of people different from ourselves in an academic, non-threatening atmosphere? In truth, this . . . cohort is the first time that I've encountered such diverse people in all my graduate courses. I am constantly amazed at the responses of some of the people in class because they are so different from my own experience and way of thinking. This is truly energizing and I am enjoying the exchange a lot.

Ethics as a Process

We have come to see the teaching of ethics as an ever-evolving process on the part of the professors as well as the students. We believe that conscious reflection about our pedagogy should enable us to be more honest with those we teach and also help us to decide if the pedagogical approaches we select are appropriate for the material to be taught. Self-reflection by professors also models for students ways to carry out their own moral self-assessments.

For instance, our students gave us excellent feedback as we modified our course. They also seemed enthusiastic about the various approaches we used. As one student pointed out, "Each assignment caused me to think about what I thought was important both as a human being and as a reflective practitioner." Another mentioned that "The journals were an excellent way of keeping track of the cognition and the developing awareness of the participants." A third student added, "this journal . . . [has] . . . allowed me to read articles and pieces much more critically. It was a necessary part of my intellectual growth."

Others reflected on the need for codes of ethics. As one student, a White male administrator, confided, "Often administrators go on 'gut feelings'. . . . This course has been somewhat difficult for me since it has forced me to think systematically and reflectively about my motives and actions with respect to values and ethics. . . ."

Although we do not advocate "one best model," in our case we did find that a 7-week block of time focusing on ethics enabled our students to move beyond their initial discomfort with the reflective nature of the class. In fact, as these students grew accustomed to this way of thinking and to the introspection so critical in this process, they began to see the merits of such an approach and many wished that there had been more time in the curriculum devoted to ethics. As one student, a female administrator in her 40s, pointed out: "At first I thought perhaps the ideas of changing one's ethics was 'unethical' and perhaps meant that you weren't 'well-grounded.' But now I think that for some people, a change in their ethics or morals shows growth and enlightenment."

This course was not easy, either or for the professors or for the students who struggled with the reflective nature of the pedagogy. As one professor who taught the class after us said, "This is a difficult course because you have to think about it after you have left it, when you go home at night. . . . It's a course that everyone in our department should teach. . . ."

A similar struggle toward understanding is reflected in the words of one of our youngest students, a suburban woman in her 20s:

> I have struggled to think in the manner that this course has forced me to. It is easier to see black and white than gray, but ethical thought doesn't permit this. A decision is only fair when all angles are explored, and all voices heard, and even then someone will always question the decision that was made. However, I know that I can be at peace with myself if I have been ethical in my thought and decision making processes.

The reflective nature of the ethics course and the discussion with peers, in both small and large group settings, led many students to mention that the ethics class had a positive effect on their doctoral cohort group. This course was taught in the spring semester of the first year of the doctoral cohort experience. What follows are samples of reflections from three very different students who saw this growth:

> I can see the impetus for thought reshaping in our discussions in class. They are provoking and, most of all, mind-changing. I find that the course is also causing our cohort members to bond in a most desirable way. Our small group discussions, though often side-tracked by extraneous banter, challenge us and cause us to divulge our innermost beliefs, feelings, and motivations. (African-American male, urban, mid-30s)

> (By) participating in our current class and experiencing the readings, I have felt a closeness to the people in our cohort that I did not have before. Perhaps it is enlightenment or there is less pressure and more cooperation than the other . . . classes which I have encountered. I like the concept of splitting into groups in order to share our moral beliefs . . . it promotes altruism, reasonable people. (White male, small-town, 40s)

> (T)his course has greatly unified our cohort. In the fall there were many instances when viewpoints were not respected and differences stood out. We were all very protective of our individual identities. However, on the night we sat in groups and worked on a common code of personal ethics, the aura of competition and individu-

ality melted and made way for a new aura of acceptance. (White female, suburban, 20s)

In Conclusion

Throughout this chapter, we stressed the importance of conversations between professors, focusing on issues such as who they are and what and how they teach. Such conversations can lead to careful content analysis of what readings and resources are privileged in the classroom. They can also help to identify what pedagogical approaches are employed to make certain that the content is delivered to all students. We feel that in-depth, thoughtful, and provocative discussions will help us to assess what voices we tend to emphasize when we teach—the voice of justice, rights, law; the voice of critique and possibilities; the voice of care, concern, connectedness; alternatively, a combination of these voices. It was also through this experience that we were able to recognize the need for an additional paradigm—the ethic of the profession.

References

American Association of University Women. (1992). *How schools shortchange girls: A study of major findings on girls and education*. Washington, DC: American Association of University Women Foundation.

American Association of University Women. (1995). *Achieving gender equity in the classroom and the campus: The next step*. Washington, DC: American Association of University Women Foundation.

American Association of School Administrators. (1981). *Statement of ethics for school administrators*. Arlington, VA: Author.

Anyon, J. (1980, Winter). Social class and the hidden curriculum of work. *Journal of Education, 162*(1), pp. 67–92.

Apple, M. W. (1988). *Teachers and texts: A political economy of class and gender relations in education*. New York: Routledge & Kegan Paul.

Ashbaugh, C. R., & Kasten, K. L. (1995). *Educational leadership: Case studies for reflective practice* (2nd ed.). White Plains, NY: Longman.

Bakhtin, M. (1981). *The dialogic imagination*. Austin: University of Texas Press.

Banks, J. A., & Banks, C. A. (1993). *Multicultural education: issues and perspectives* (2nd ed.). Boston: Allyn & Bacon.

Barth, R. J. (1990). *Improving schools from within: Teachers, parents, and principals can make the difference*. San Francisco: Jossey-Bass.

Beauchamp, T. L., & Childress, J. F. (1984). Morality, ethics and ethical theories. In P. Sola (Ed.), *Ethics, education, and administrative decisions: A book of readings* (pp. 39–67). New York: Peter Lang.

Beck, L. G. (1994). *Reclaiming educational administration as a caring profession*. New York: Teachers' College Press.

Beck, L. G., & Murphy, J. (1994a). *Ethics in educational leadership programs: An expanding role*. Thousand Oaks, CA: Corwin Press.

Beck L. G., & Murphy, J. (1994b, April 6). *A deeper analysis: Examining courses devoted to ethics*. Paper presented at the annual meeting of the American Educational Research Association, New Orleans.

111

Beck, L. G., Murphy, J., & Associates (1997). *Ethics in educational leadership programs: Emerging models.* Columbia, MO: The University Council for Educational Administration.

Begley, P. T., & Johansson, O. (1998, July). The values of school administration: Preferences, ethics, & conflicts. *Journal of School Leadership, 9*(4), 399–422.

Belenky, M. F., Clinchy, B. M., Goldberger, N. R., & Tarule, J. M. (1986). *Women's ways of knowing.* New York: Basic Books.

Bennett, W. J. (1989). *James Madison high school: A curriculum for American students.* Washington, DC: U.S. Department of Education.

Bloom, A. (1987). *The closing of the American mind.* New York: Simon & Schuster.

Board of Education, Island Trees Union Free School District No. 26 v. Pico, 457 U.S. 853 (1981).

Bolman, L. G., & Deal, T. E. (1991). *Reframing organizations: Artistry, choice, and leadership.* San Francisco: Jossey-Bass.

Bourdieu, P. (1977). Cultural reproduction and social reproduction. In J. Karabel & A. H. Halsey (Eds.), *Power and ideology in education* (pp. 487–511). New York: Oxford.

Bowles, S., & Gintis, H. (1988). *Democracy and capitalism.* New York: Basic Books.

Boyer, E. L. (1990). *Scholarship Reconsidered: Priorities of the Professoriate.* San Francisco: Jossey-Bass Inc.

Buber, M. (1965). Education. In M. Buber (Ed.), *Between man and man* (pp. 83–103). New York: Macmillan.

Cambron-McCabe, N. H., & Foster, W. (1994). A paradigm shift: Implications for the preparation of school leaders. In T. Mulkeen, N. H. Cambron-McCabe, & B. Anderson (Eds.), *Democratic leadership: The changing context of administrative preparation* (pp. 49–60). Norwood, NJ: Ablex.

Capper, C. A. (1993). Educational administration in a pluralistic society: A multiparadigm approach. In C. A. Capper (Ed.), *Educational administration in a pluralistic society* (pp. 7–35). Albany: State University of New York Press.

Carnoy, M., & Levin, H. (1985). *Schooling and work in the democratic state.* Stanford, CA: Stanford University Press.

Comer, J. P. (1988). Is "parenting" essential to good teaching? *NEA Today, 6,* 34–40.

Cooper, J. M. (1995). *Teachers' problem solving: A casebook of award-winning teaching cases.* Boston: Allyn & Bacon.

Cornfield v. Consolidated School District. No. 230, 991 F.2d 1316 (7th Cir. 1993).

Crittenden, B. (1984). Morality, ethics and ethical theories. In P. Sola (Ed.), *Ethics, education, and administrative decisions: A book of readings* (pp. 15–38). New York: Peter Lang.

Cushner, K., McClelland, A., & Safford, P. (1992). *Human diversity in education: An integrative approach.* New York: McGraw Hill.

Delgado, R. (1995). *Critical race theory: The cutting edge.* Philadelphia: Temple University Press.

DeMitchell, T. A. (1993). Private lives: Community control vs. professional autonomy. *West's Educational Law Quarterly, 2*(2), 218–226.

Dewey, J. (1902). *The school and society.* Chicago: University of Chicago Press.

Duke, D., & Grogan, M. (1997). The moral and ethical dimensions of leadership. In L. G. Beck, J. Murphy, & Associates (Eds.), *Ethics in educational leadership programs: Emerging models* (pp. 141–160). Columbia, MO: University Council for Educational Administration.

Fine, M. (1991). *Framing dropouts.* Albany: State University of New York Press.

Fishkin, J. (1983). *Justice, equal opportunity, and the family.* New Haven, CT: Yale University Press.

Foster, W. (1986) *Paradigms and promises: New approaches to educational administration.* Buffalo, NY: Prometheus Books.

Foucault, M. (1983). On the genealogy of ethics: An overview of work in progress. In H. L. Dreyfus & P. Rabinow (Eds.), *Michel Foucault: Beyond structuralism and hermeneutics* (2nd ed., pp. 229–252). Chicago: University of Chicago Press.

Freire, P. (1970) *Pedagogy of the oppressed.* (M. B. Ramos, Trans.). New York: Continuum.

Gilligan, C. (1982). *In a different voice.* Cambridge, MA: Harvard University Press.

Gilligan, C., Ward, J., & Taylor, J. (1988). *Mapping the moral domain: A contribution of women's thinking to psychology and education.* Cambridge, MA: Harvard University Graduate School of Education.

Giroux, H. A. (1988). *Schooling and the struggle for public life: Critical pedagogy in the modern age.* Minneapolis: The University of Minnesota Press.

Giroux, H. A. (Ed.). (1991). *Postmodernism, feminism, and cultural politics: Redrawing educational boundaries.* Albany, NY: State University of New York Press.

Giroux, H. A. (1992). *Border crossings: Cultural workers and the politics of education.* New York: Routledge.

Giroux, H. A. (1994). Educational leadership and school administrators: Rethinking the meaning of democratic public culture. In T. Mulkeen, N. H. Cambron-McCabe, & B. Anderson (Eds.), *Democratic leadership: The changing context of administrative preparation* (pp. 31–47). Norwood, NJ: Ablex.

Giroux, H. A., & Aronowitz, S. (1985) *Education under siege.* South Hadley, MA: Bergin & Garvey.

Glaser, J. W. (1994). *Three realms of ethics: Individual, institutional, societal.* Kansas City, MO: Sheed & Ward.

Gollnick, D. M., & Chinn, P. C. (1994). *Multicultural education in a pluralistic society.* Columbus, OH: Merrill.

Goodlad, J. I., Soder, R., & Sirotnik, K. A. (Eds.). (1990). *The moral dimension of teaching.* San Francisco: Jossey-Bass.

Greene, M. (1978). *Landscapes of learning.* New York: Teachers College Press.

Greene, M. (1988). *The dialectic of freedom.* New York: Teachers College Press.

Greenfield, W. D. (1993). Articulating values and ethics in administrator preparation. In C. Capper (Ed.), *Educational administration in a pluralistic society* (pp. 267–287). Albany, NY: State University of New York Press.

Greenwood, G. E., & Filmer, H. T. (1997). *Professional core cases for teacher decision-making.* Upper Saddle River, NJ: Prentice-Hall.

Guthrie, J. W. (1990). The evolution of educational management: Eroding myths and emerging models. In B. Mitchell & L. Cunningham (Eds.), *Educational leadership and changing contexts of families, communities, and schools: Eighty-ninth yearbook of the National Society for the Study of Education* (pp. 210–231). Chicago: University of Chicago Press.

Hersh, R. H., Paolitto, D. P., & Reimer, J. (1979). *Promoting moral growth: From Piaget to Kohlberg.* New York: Longman.

Hirsch, E. D. (1987). *Cultural literacy.* Boston: Houghton Mifflin.

Hirst, P. H. (1974). *Moral education in a secular society.* London: University of London Press.

Hodgkinson, H. L. (1992). *A demographic look at tomorrow.* Washington, DC: Institute for Education Leadership.

Hoffman, N. (1981). *Woman's "true" profession: Voices from the history of teaching.* Old Westbury, NY: The Feminist Press.

Hutchings, P. (1998). Building on progress. *AAHE Bulletin, 50*(6), 10–11.

Hyman, I. A., & Snook, P. A. (1999). *Dangerous schools: What we can do about the physical and emotional abuse of our children.* San Francisco: Jossey-Bass.

Interstate School Leaders Licensure Consortium (ISLLC). (1996). *Standards for school leaders.* Washington, DC: Author.

Jensen, A. (1969). "How Much Can We Boost IQ and Scholastic Achievement." *Harvard Educational Review, 39*(1), 1–123.

Katz, M. S., Noddings, N., & Strike, K. A. (Eds.). (1999). *Justice and caring: The search for common ground in education.* New York: Teachers' College Press.

Kirschmann, R. E. (1996). *Educational administration: A collection of case studies.* Englewood Cliffs, NJ: Prentice-Hall.

Kohlberg, L. (1981). *The philosophy of moral development: moral stages and the idea of justice* (Vol. 1). San Francisco, CA: Harper & Row.

Lareau, A. (1987). Social class differences in family school relationships: The importance of cultural capital. *Sociology of Education, 60,* 73–85.

Lebacqz, K. (1985). *Professional ethics: Power and paradox.* Nashville, TN: Abingdon.

Maher, F. A., & Tetreault, M. K. T. (1994). *The feminist classroom.* New York: Basic Books.

Marshall, C. (1995). Imagining leadership. *Educational Administration Quarterly, 31*(3), 484–492.

McBroom v. Board of Education, District No. 205, 144 Ill. App. 3d 463, 98 Ill. 864, 494 N.E.2d 1191 (1986).

Merseth, K. K. (1997). *Case studies in educational administration.* New York: Addison Wesley Longman.

Mertz, N. T. (1997). Knowing and doing: Exploring the ethical life of educational leaders. In L. G. Beck, J. Murphy, & Associates (Eds.), *Ethics in educational leadership programs: Emerging models* (pp. 77–94). Columbia, MO: University Council for Educational Administration.

Morholt, E., Brandwein, P. F., & Alexander, J. (1966). *A source-book for the biological sciences* (2nd ed.). New York: Harcourt, Brace & World.

Morrison v. Board of Education, 1 Cal. 3d 214, 82 Cal. Rptr. 175, 461 P.2d 375 (1969).

Nash, R. J. (1996). *"Real world" ethics: Frameworks for educators and human service professionals.* New York: Teachers College Press.

Noddings, N. (1984). *Caring: A feminine approach to ethics and moral education.* Berkeley: University of California Press.

Noddings, N. (1992). *The challenge to care in schools: An alternative approach to education.* New York: Teachers College Press.

Oakes, J. (1993). Tracking, inequality, and the rhetoric of reform: Why schools don't change. In S. H. Shapiro & D. E. Purpel (Eds.), *Critical social issues in American education: Toward the 21st century* (pp. 85–102). White Plains, NY: Longman.

O'Keefe, J. (1997). Preparing ethical leaders for equitable schools. In L. G. Beck, J. Murphy, & Associates (Eds.), *Ethics in educational leadership programs: Emerging models* (pp. 161–187). Columbia, MO: University Council for Educational Administration.

Parker, L., & Shapiro, J. P. (1993). The context of educational administration and social class. In C. A. Capper (Ed.). *Educational administration in a pluralistic society* (pp. 36–65). Albany: State University of New York Press.

Pennsylvania Code of Professional Practice and Conduct for Educators, 22 Pa.Code, §§ 235.1–235.11 (1992).

People v. Dukes, 580 N.Y.S.2d 850 (N.Y. Criminal Court 1992).

Peters, R. S. (1973). *Reason and compassion.* London: Routledge & Kegan Paul.

Plessy v. Ferguson, 163 U.S. 537 (1896).

Purpel, D. E. (1989). *The moral and spiritual crisis in education: A curriculum for justice and compassion in education.* New York: Bergin & Garvey.

Purpel, D. E., & Shapiro, S. (1995) *Beyond liberation and excellence: Reconstructing the public discourse on education.* Westport, CT: Bergin & Garvey.

Ravitch, D., & Finn, C. E. (1987). *What do our 17-year-olds know?* New York: Harper & Row.

Roland Martin, J. (1993). Becoming educated: A journey of alienation or integration? In S. H. Shapiro & D. E. Purpel (Eds.), *Critical social issues in American education: Toward the 21st century* (pp. 137–148). White Plains, NY: Longman.

Sergiovanni, T. J. (1992). *Moral leadership: Getting to the heart of school improvement.* San Francisco: Jossey-Bass.

Sewell, T. E., DuCette, J. P., & Shapiro, J. P. (1998). Educational assessment and diversity. In N. M. Lambert & B. L. McCombs (Eds.), *How students learn: Reforming schools through learner-centered education* (pp. 311–338). Washington, DC: American Psychological Association.

Shapiro, H. S., & Purpel, D. E. (Eds.). (1993). *Critical social issues in American education: Toward the 21st century.* New York: Longman.

Shapiro, J. P., Sewell, T. E., & DuCette, J. P. (1995). *Reframing diversity in education.* Lancaster, PA: Technomic.

Shapiro, J. P., Sewell, T. E., DuCette, J., & Myrick, H. (1997, March). *Socio-cultural and school factors in achievement: Lessons from tuition guarantee programs.* Paper presented at the annual meeting of the American Educational Research Association, Chicago.

Shapiro, J. P., & Smith-Rosenberg, C. (1989). The "other voices" in contemporary ethical dilemmas: The value of the new scholarship on women in the teaching of ethics. *Women's Studies International Forum, 12*(2), 199–211.

Shapiro, J. P., & Stefkovich, J. A. (1997). The ethics of justice, critique and care: Preparing educational administrators to lead democratic and diverse schools. In J. Murphy, L. G. Beck, & Associates (Eds.), *Ethics in educational administration: Emerging models* (pp. 109–140). Columbia, MO: University Council for Educational Administration.

Shapiro, J. P., & Stefkovich, J. A. (1998). Dealing with dilemmas in a morally polarized era: The conflicting ethical codes of educational leaders. *Journal for a Just and Caring Education, 4*(2), 117–141.

Shulman, L. (1997). The advancement of teaching. *AAHE Bulletin, 50*(1), 3–7.

Sleeter, C. E., & Grant, C. A. (1988). *Making choices for multicultural education: Five approaches to race, class, and gender.* New York: Macmillan.

Starratt, R. J. (1991). Building an ethical school: A theory for practice in educational leadership. *Educational Administration Quarterly, 27*(2), 185–202.

Starratt, R. J. (1994a). *Building an ethical school.* London: Falmer Press.

Starratt, R. J. (1994b). Afterword. In L. G. Beck & J. Murphy (Eds.), *Ethics in educational leadership programs: An expanding role* (pp. 100–103). Thousand Oaks, CA: Corwin Press.

Starratt, R. J. (1994c, April 6). *Preparing administrators for ethical practice: State of the art.* Paper presented at the annual meeting of the American Educational Research Association, New Orleans.

Stefkovich, J. A., & Guba, G. J. (1998). School violence, school reform, and the fourth amendment in public schools. *International Journal of Educational Reform, 7*(3), 217–225.

Stefkovich, J. A., & O'Brien, G. J. (2000). Students' fourth amendment rights and school officials' responsibilities: Implications for law and practice. *Thresholds in Education, 20.*

Stefkovich, J. A., & Shapiro, J. P. (1994). Personal and professional ethics for educational administrators. *Review Journal of Philosophy and Social Science, 20*(1&2), 157–186.

Strike, K. A. (1991). The moral role of schooling in liberal democratic society. In G. Grant (Ed.), *Review of Research in Education* (pp. 413–483). Washington, DC: American Educational Research Association.

Strike, K. A., Haller, E. J., & Soltis, J. F. (1988). *The ethics of school administration.* New York: Teachers College Press.

Strike, K. A., Haller, E. J., & Soltis, J. F. (1998). *The ethics of school administration* (2nd ed.). New York: Teachers College Press.

Strike, K., & Soltis, J. F. (1992). *The ethics of teaching* (2nd ed.). New York: Teachers College Press.

Tek Lum, W. (1987). *Chinese hot pot.* Honolulu, HI: Bamboo Ridge Press.

Texas Administrative Code, Title 19, § 177.1 (1998).

Tyack, D. B. (1974). *The one-best system: A history of urban education.* Cambridge, MA: Harvard University Press.

Utley, C. A., & Obiakor, F. E. (July, 1995). *Scientific and methodological concerns in research perspectives for multicultural learners.* Paper presented at the Office of Special Education Project Direction Conference, Washington, DC.

Weis, L., & Fine, M. (1993). *Beyond silenced voices: Class, race, & gender in U.S. schools.* Albany: State University of New York Press.

Welch, S. (1991). An ethic of solidarity and difference. In H. Giroux (Ed.), *Postmodernism, feminism, and cultural politics: Redrawing educational boundaries* (pp. 83–99). Albany: State University of New York Press.

Willower, D. J., & Licata, J. W. (1997). *Values and valuation in the practice of education administration.* Thousand Oaks, CA: Corwin Press.

Willower, D. J. (1999, October). *Work on values in educational administration: Some observations.* Paper presented at the annual meeting of the University Council for Educational Administration Center for the Study of Ethnics and Leadership, Charlottesville, VA.

Witherell, C., & Noddings, N. (1991). *Stories lives tell: Narrative and dialogue in education.* New York: Teachers College Press.

Wong, S. C. (1993). Promises, pitfalls, and principles of text selection in curricular diversification: The Asian-American case. In T. Perry & J. W. Fraser (Eds.), *Freedom's plow: Teaching in the multicultural classroom,* (pp. 109–120). New York: Routledge.

Young, I. M. (1990). *Justice and the politics of difference.* Princeton, NJ: Princeton University Press.

Zangwill, I. (1910). *The melting-pot, 1909.* New York: Macmillan.

Author Index

117

Subject Index

About the Contributors

Joan Poliner Shapiro is a professor of Educational Administration in the Educational Leadership and Policy Studies Department and Associate Dean for Research and Development at Temple University's College of Education. She previously served as Associate Director of the College of Education's Center on Research in Education (CoRE) at Temple and Co-Director of Women's Studies Program at the University of Pennsylvania. In addition, she was a junior high and high school teacher of social studies in the United States and United Kingdom, and a supervisor of intern teachers. Dr. Shapiro holds a doctorate in Educational Administration from the University of Pennsylvania. Her research interests include ethics in education and diversity issues, with a special focus on gender, participatory evaluation, and feminist assessment. She has co-authored a book entitled *Reframing Diversity in Education* and has published numerous journal articles and book chapters in her areas of interest.

Jacqueline A. Stefkovich is a professor of school law at The Pennsylvania State University, Department of Education Policy Studies. She was previously professor and coordinator of the Educational Administration Program at Temple University where she taught courses in education law and ethics. She holds a doctoral degree in Administration, Planning, and Social Policy from Harvard University's Graduate School of Education and a JD from the University of Pennsylvania Law School. She has worked as a public school guidance counselor and teacher, a state-level administrator, and a consultant for three regional educational laboratories. Dr. Stefkovich's research interests focus on students' rights and administra-

123

tors' responsibilities under the 4th Amendment to the U.S. Constitution. She has written extensively on this topic and has received funding from the Spencer Foundation for this research.

****

Gregory Allen has been involved in education for 21 years as a music educator. He received his BA from Lincoln University and his master's degree from West Chester University. He is a doctoral candidate in the Department of Educational Leadership and Policy Studies at Temple University. Mr. Allen's research explores character through the perceptions and attitudes of ninth grade urban high school students. He is convinced that secondary educators can help to cause paradigm shifts among troubled teenage youth regarding civility and sound moral character.

Kimberly D. Callahan has been a classroom teacher for 15 years. She currently teaches high school biology in Pennsylvania. She received her BS degree from Ursinus College and her master's in science education and doctorate in educational administration from Temple University. Her dissertation consisted of an action research study of the integration between an academic high school and a technology career center in a suburban setting. Dr. Callahan has conducted several workshops on her primary research interest, the school-to-work system.

Joseph A. Castellucci is the principal of Lower Cape May Regional High School in Cape May, New Jersey. Prior to becoming principal he was an assistant principal, and before that, a teacher of high school social studies. He received his bachelor's degree from Penn State University and a master's degree from Jersey City State College. He is pursuing his doctorate degree at Temple University where he is writing a dissertation about school change.

Lynn A. Cheddar is an instructional support teacher in the Saucon Valley School District in Hellertown, Pennsylvania. Previously she taught third grade for 7 years. After receiving a master's of education in reading from Kutztown University, she enrolled at Temple University where she is currently pursuing a doctorate in educational administration. She has conducted workshops and staff development at various educational conferences and in school districts in Pennsylvania.

Robert L. Crawford holds an EdD in educational administration and policy studies from Temple University. Dr. Crawford's dissertation, which focused on the influence of character education programs on the development of student morality, received the prestigious Ralph D. Owen Award from Temple's chapter of Phi Delta Kappa. Dr. Crawford, who has held positions such as Director of Special Education Programs and Assistant Principal for a K–8 public school district, is currently director of the Psychiatric Emergency Screening and Crisis Center at Underwood Memorial Hospital in Woodbury, New Jersey. Dr. Crawford continues to conduct research and training in the fields of moral development and character education, school violence, and related mental health issues.

James C. Dyson teaches sixth, seventh, and eighth grade music classes in Swiftwater, Pennsylvania. He received a BS from West Chester Pennsylvania University, elementary education certification, a master's in secondary education and elementary/secondary principal certification from East Stroudsburg University. He is presently pursuing a doctorate in educational administration at Temple University.

Patricia A. L. Ehrensal is a doctoral candidate in the Educational Leadership and Policy Studies Department at Temple University. Her dissertation, *Talking About Drugs and Violence: Dominant Elite National Discourses in a Comparative Perspective,* deconstructs legal documents which crystalize the dominant elite national discourses surrounding drugs and violence in schools in the United States and England. Her research interests include critical theory, poststructuralism, organizational theory, education, law, and policy. Ms. Ehrensal has presented papers at several conferences in the United States and England. She has also published articles in *The Journal for a Just and Caring Education,* and *Religion and Public Education.* In addition to her doctoral work and research, Ms. Ehrensal served as a school director on the Pottstown Pennsylvania School Board, and is a member of that district's strategic planning committee.

Loree P. Guthrie is a middle school principal at Pocono Mountain School District in Swiftwater, Pennsylvania. Prior to entering the field of administration, she taught Advanced Placement senior English for 15 years. She is presently involved in an educational partnership, housed within her school, for professional development with East Stroudsburg University. Dr. Guthrie received her doctorate in educational administration from Temple University.

James K. Krause is a former public school teacher and administrator of special education. He is currently an assistant professor in the Department of Exceptionality Program at Bloomsburg University of Pennsylvania, where he coordinates the Special Education Administration Certification Program. His research interests include inclusive practices for students with disabilities, special education administration, instructional methodology for students with disabilities, and pre-service teacher training. He holds an Ed.D. degree from the Educational Leadership and Policy Studies Department at Temple University.

Patricia A. Maloney is the supervisor of student support services for the Ephrata Area School District in Ephrata, Pennsylvania. She is a former classroom teacher, high school guidance counselor, and assistant high school principal. She received her undergraduate and masters' degrees from Millersville University and her doctorate in educational administration from Temple University. Dr. Maloney's research interests are in the areas of alternative education and at-risk youth. Most recently, she developed and led an alternative high school for at-risk students.

Beatrice H. Mickey is an administrator in the school district of Philadelphia. She is a former middle school principal. She earned her master's in English education and her doctorate in educational administration at Temple University. Dr. Mickey's area of expertise includes school organization and management and instructional leadership. She has a broad teaching background with experience from the elementary school level as a reading specialist, to the graduate level as an adjunct professor of education. Her research interests encompass instructional leadership at the secondary level, student-centered instructional practices, and the role of the teacher as a facilitator of learning.

G. Michaele O'Brien is an advanced doctoral student in the Department of Educational Leadership and Policy Studies at Temple University in Philadelphia, Pennsylvania. She is the recipient of a university fellowship for her graduate work in the area of educational policy. She has co-authored numerous articles, appearing in publications such as *Education and Urban Society, Illinois School Law Quarterly, School Business Affairs and Education Law Reporter.* Currently, Ms. O'Brien is All-School Coordinator at The New School of Lancaster, a private institution for Grades pre-K through 8.

Leon D. Poeske is a school administrator in Bucks County, Pennsylvania. He is completing his doctoral dissertation at Temple University on the secondary school accreditation process. Mr. Poeske taught mathematics for 11 years at the middle and high school levels. He also served as a Peace Corps volunteer in West Africa.

John A. Schlegel has been involved in education for 22 years as a teacher and administrator. He received his BS in secondary education from Kutztown State College, his master's in guidance from Millersville State University, and his doctorate in educational administration from Temple University. He is currently the principal at Swatara Junior High School in the Central Dauphin School District near Harrisburg, Pennsylvania.

Spencer S. Stober is Dean of Arts and Sciences at Alvernia College in Reading, Pennsylvania. He recently earned his doctorate in educational leadership and policy studies from Temple University. Dr. Stober retains his faculty status at Alvernia College as an associate professor of biology where he has been teaching genetics and general biology since 1985. He previously taught science for 15 years in the Governor Mifflin School District in Shillington, Pennsylvania.

David J. Traini has been in public education since 1978. He holds a bachelor's degree in philosophy from Princeton University and a master's in educational administration from Glassboro State College (now Rowan University). He spent 11 years as a physical science teacher before joining the ranks of administration. He is currently an administrator at Cumberland Regional High School in Seabrook, one of the first schools in New Jersey to move to block scheduling.

William W. Watts has been an educator for the past 20 years and has also served as an athletic director. He is actively involved with his school's Student Assistance Program, Blue Ribbon Schools program, and many other school organizations. Dr. Watts earned his BS in Health and Physical Education from the University of Pittsburgh, MA in educational administration from Rider College, and EdD in educational administration and policy studies from Temple University. His dissertation study examines school violence.

Deborah Weaver is the coordinating elementary principal in Elizabethtown, Pennsylvania. She received her BS from West Chester University, MEd degrees from both Penn State, Harrisburg and Shippensburg Universities, and her doctorate from Temple University. As a 25-year veteran in the field of education, her involvement in her profession has included classroom teaching at both the elementary and middle school levels, active participation in educationally related organizations, and facilitation of workshops on curriculum, staff development, and nongraded education. She has also given presentations on various topics, but most often on nongraded multiage classrooms based on her dissertation research.